The Polishing Cloth

Tenth Edition

Georgia Perimeter College

Barbara Mortimer~Jeanette Gibson-Allen~ Michael Hall

Editors

KENDALL/HUNT PUBLISHING COMPANY
4050 Westmark Drive   Dubuque, Iowa 52002

Page 65 song lyrics of "Pass You By"

Words and Music by Michael McCary, Nathan Morris, Wanya Morris and Shawn Stockman.
Copyright © 2000 by Black Panther Publishing Co., Vanderpool Publishing, Aynaw Publishing,
Shawn Patrick Publishing and Ensign Music Corporation. Internal Copyright Secured.
All Rights Reserved.

Cover photography by Emmanuelle Joseph

ISBN 0-7872-8411-4

Printed in the United States of America
10 9 8 7 6 5 4 3 2 1

Contents

English Composition I
(ENGL 1101)

In-Class Essays

Essay Outlines

Photographs

Preface

Now in its sixteenth year, *The Polishing Cloth* publishes examples of the best student writing from courses at Georgia Perimeter College. These examples of student essays offer accessible, engaging, and up-to-date models of writing for assignments in composition and literature courses, including English as a Second Language and Learning Support. The modes of writing range from autobiographical narration to analysis of literature, with several examples of the research paper using MLA documentation style. As in past editions, *The Polishing Cloth* also offers examples of actual exit exam essays for ENGL 0099 and actual Regents' Test essays. One difference this year is that there are more examples of literary analysis, while some rhetorical modes such as cause-and-effect are not included. This editorial choice reflects the type of work submitted this year; while numerous examples of narration and literary analysis were submitted, very few essays were submitted in other traditional modes. One possible explanation is that essays of those types are not assigned as often as in the past. Whatever the reason, we have decided to make room for more outstanding essays in the categories that drew the largest response.

The selection process worked the same way this year as it has in years past. With their instructor's encouragement, students who had excelled on a writing assignment submitted their work to *The Polishing Cloth*, and the editorial board, comprised of college-wide Humanities Division faculty, considered each submission for publication. This year we received 172 essays. The essays included here in the tenth edition were selected to show effective writing in a variety of modes common to English courses; they were also selected for their potential to stimulate classroom discussion regarding their form and content. We hope that students and instructors will enjoy analyzing what makes these essays work and considering, too, what might make them work even better. The essays are not meant to illustrate some ideal of rhetorical perfection; rather, they are meant to interest and inspire students and give them confidence to tackle similar assignments themselves.

These essays may also serve to remind us that good writing derives from having something to say on a subject that one cares about. See, for example, Elena Resiga's essay on growing up in Romania, Daniel Proto's essay on the need to reform the Electoral College, or Santina Bennett's essay on the characters in Hemingway's story "Hills Like White Elephants." The knowledge, experiences, and beliefs of the writer drive the writing, helping to shape not only the thesis but also the tone, the organization, and the style—that is, every aspect of the essay's form. These essays capture the diversity of student voices at Georgia Perimeter College, where people from all over the world pursue their education together. This collection attempts to convey the richness of experience of our campus community.

As always, we owe thanks to many people, without whom this book would not be possible. We thank President Jacquelyn Belcher for her support of *The Polishing Cloth*. Dean of Academic Services Ron Swofford has been a champion of *The Polishing Cloth* since its inception; his wisdom and encouragement have sustained it over the years. He and the entire Literary Publications Executive Board have given us outstanding support and advice. David Tart of Kendall-Hunt Publishing provided crucial assistance in preparing the manuscript for publication and coordinating the various stages of the publication process. Thanks are also due to Sandra Rosseter for her assistance in locating outstanding Regents' Test essays and to Margee Bright-Ragland and Shirley Cox of the Fine Arts Department for their assistance in coordinating the student photography that so enhances this edition. And finally, we want to thank the faculty and students at the College who have demonstrated their commitment to writing well as a foundation of higher education.

Barbara Mortimer, Jeanette Gibson-Allen,
Michael Hall

The Polishing Cloth

Editions held by Dunwoody Campus Library

Vol. 1, No. 1	Spring 1985
Vol. 1, No.2	Fall and Winter 1985-1986
Vol. 2, No. 1	Spring and Summer 1985-1986
Vol. 2, No. 2	Fall and Winter 1986-1987
Vol. 3, No. 1	Spring and Summer 1986-1987
Vol. 3, No. 2	Fall and Winter 1987-1988
Vol. 4, No. 1	Spring/Summer 1988
Vol. 5	1988-1989
Vol. 6	1990
Vol. 7	1991
First edition	1992
Second edition	1993
Third edition	1994
Fourth edition	1995
Fifth edition	1996
Sixth edition	1997
Seventh edition	1998
Eighth edition	1999
Ninth edition	2000
Tenth edition	2001

How and Where I Learned To Read

By Elena Resiga

ENSL 0095: Narration

As a child, I was dying of curiosity. If there was an interdict against something, my curiosity grew bigger and bigger. When I was born, my country Romania was under a Communist regime, so I "enjoyed" many interdictions. I often asked, "Why can't I listen to Radio Free Europe?" or "Why can't we visit another country?" or "Why can't we read something about the United States or Australia?" I wanted to experience things. I wanted to read and to think for myself.

At five years old I saw an uncle smoking, and my father told me that it is really bad to smoke, but he forgot to tell me why. So the next day I went to my uncle's packet of cigarettes, I stole a big one, and I went to smoke in a storage area where my father kept gasoline, oils, and cans of paint. After I inhaled once, I was so dizzy that I couldn't see my father at the door. I was spanked so hard because of stealing, smoking, and smoking in a place with a danger of fire. This was an experience with bad consequences, but my curiosity made me achieve a lot of good things, too.

At the same age I had my smoking experience, I didn't have any friends to play with because everybody went to school. They were older, and they made a big deal about school, so I wanted to go, too. I could not go to school because of my age, and all my friends laughed because I had to stay home playing by myself. I cried, I made scenes, and finally I was allowed to go with my older cousin one day of the week. She was in the third grade, and I had a lot of fun with those older kids. I didn't know how to read, and when she did her homework, I learned the alphabet. At seven years old I knew how to read and write, and I was the best of my generation when I started the first grade.

My curiosity was diminished because I was bored, but I discovered poetry by Eugen Mirea and Stelian Filip and many other writers of whom Romanian communism was proud. In two years of school I was the best "Pioneer" (future communist) that my country ever had. After a while my parents realized what kind of child they could have, and my mother told me one day about writers who "wrote better than all f...ing communists put together." I was surprised to hear my mom, who was a lady, talking like this. Later, I found out that my mother's father was in jail because he had a library. In 1945 the communists came and burned all his books, took everything from his house for "communal use," withdrew everything from his bank, and put him in jail. I didn't know him, but I was raised by my father's parents who lost two water mills and were forced to grow two pigs every year for "Communist Romanian Community."

After the day my mother told me about so many good writers, she told me where I could read about them. Every day after school I took the train for thirty minutes and walked two miles just to read good books. My grandparents were living at that time in a small village on the mountainside. The village had three hundred inhabitants, and the sheriff knew the priest, the priest knew the teacher, and everybody could talk freely. I discovered Stendhal, Poe, and Hemingway; I read about Mircea Eliade, the famous historian of world religions who left the country because of communism and taught History of Religion in Chicago. Some people knew I spent all my vacations there, and I even had to read my books in the basement. My grandparents' neighbors came after dark to listen to my stories, and I had to read aloud for everyone.

The tragic accident happened when somebody told the county police what was going on. Early one morning, the sheriff came to my grandma and told her that she would have a big search in twenty minutes. In the house there was only one book at a time, or sometimes people lent me just pages. Everything was fine, but my grandma was so afraid and took the book and burned it in the stove. I don't know what the writer or the title of the book was, but I have been looking for that book ever since. I was really mad at my grandma, but after they finished the search, I agreed with her, because everywhere and everything was upside down. I didn't read for a while, but I did discover God, and I knew that somebody was above Ceausescu.

Ceausescu and his wife were killed by Romanians on Christmas Day in 1989. The Romanian people had almost forgotten about him, but the "democratic-communists" came and life got worse. You have everything available now but money. Romanians, like the Russians, went on the streets calling for communism back. I left my country, and I am reading my books in such a frenzy now; I know that I will never go back nor would I want communism back, the communism that made my grandma burn the book I am still trying to find.

The First Home of My Own

By Ke Ma

ENSL 0095: In-class essay, narration

Over time, when I hear "home," my first impression is of a small, two-room apartment filled with love, laughing, whispers, and tears—the first home ever for my ex-girlfriend and me. I will never forget the time we spent together in that place.

It was two years ago. We decided to rent an apartment on our own. We were deeply in love. I was 18. She was 19. We were both independent, but it was still very hard for us to make our own place. We were very excited at first. We spent days driving around the city to buy all kinds of stuff which would make the apartment like a home. We bought mattresses, kitchen stuff, a TV set, a VCR, tables, chairs, and everything we could buy on our budget. We didn't even know how to use most of the things we bought. It took us about a week to set everything up. We were very happy because that was our own place. I would never forget the smile on her face when we were done. We spent the next ten months together. I remember that nothing would make me feel happier than when she liked my cooking; nothing would make me feel more grateful than when she took care of me when I was sick. We went to school together; we went to work together; we laughed together; we cried together. Two souls became one. She thought we would never be apart. So did I.

I will never forgive the biggest mistake I made when I decided to leave. It was the time when my father's company went bankrupt. My family strongly ordered me to go to Atlanta to live with my aunts. Although I claimed I could support myself, my family's voice was very strong. Finally, I chickened out, even though I saw the tears from her eyes. She was very disappointed in me. Her heart and love were dying because I would give her up for my family. She was suffering because I couldn't make up my mind. I didn't realize it until six months after we broke up. When the time came, I helped her move to a new apartment. I remember the last night we spent at that home. We didn't say anything to each other. I felt ashamed and scared to tell her my feeling: "I love you, but I have to leave." I was so weak. We built this home together. We lived in this place, enjoyed love and harmony. I destroyed it.

In the next five months we were on the phone at least one hour a day; we visited each other twice. It was painful when she felt lonely and cried on the phone, and I didn't know what to do. I will never forget the tears from her disappointed eyes the last time I took off from Salt Lake City. Her heart was being completely destroyed by me. I wanted her to come with me, but she couldn't afford the expense. I wanted to stay with her but was too weak to fight with my family. I didn't know what to do. We couldn't afford two hours' difference in time zone and two thousand miles distance in our relationship anymore. I still loved her with all my soul, but for her good and mine, we broke up after that.

I did get a better chance in Atlanta. I got my green card. I got a better job. I make more money now than I did before. There are lots of good schools for me to choose from. I did live with my aunt for a year before her family went to China. I am alone most of the time. I feel lonely because I lost my best friend. When I face myself and look at the pictures we took in that "home" at night, a silent tear will drop from my heart. Then I smile with tears because I see my home—a place that was not so clean, a place that had sweet kisses, warm hugs, and joyful tears. It was a place filled with love. It was a place filled with love and my heart.

Ethiopa and the Italian Invasion

By Meseret Demissie

ENSL 0090: Definition

Topic: How does your country's identity reflect your identity?

My country, Ethiopia, is located at the horn of Africa. Ethiopia has been an attractive target throughout history for many European colonists. Italy invaded Ethiopia in 1935, but our great-grandfathers, and to some extent our great-grandmothers, too, paid with their lives to protect our country from enemies. Moreover, our grandparents preserved our culture, language, and traditions for the next generation.

Italy invaded Ethiopia in 1935, and the war took place for almost seven years. The enemy was, of course, prepared in every aspect, but for our people it was unexpected. Italy attacked us from the air and on the ground with tanks and with all other kinds of sophisticated weapons, whereas Ethiopians were fighting just with their traditional weapons, spears and shields.

The Ethiopians fought bravely because they knew and still know that there is no life without a sovereign country. The men fought at the front, and most of the women stayed home and took care of the children and organized food supplies to send to the front. They worked hand-in-hand to protect our country.

This war brought everybody together, and there were no tribal differences, or better, they were ignored for that period of time. Everybody in the country fought and worked for the unity of Ethiopia.   There was no "Gondera," "Guraga," "Tigira," or "Oromo," which means that everybody saw himself or herself just as an Ethiopian and forgot for the time being their small clans. This unity was very positive, and, amazingly, I learned from it.

Ethiopia is the only African country that has never been colonized throughout history. My country kept its culture, traditions, and language despite the invasion of many European countries, such as Italy, as I mentioned above, England, and Portugal, who tried to invade our country in the 15th century. We have our own language and traditions that one will never see anywhere else and that we are proud of.

I think the new generation can learn a lot from the invasions and wars Ethiopia has experienced through time. Unity, hope, and courage are very important for a country to withstand invasion or similar kinds of problems. To see Ethiopia united is for me a dream come true. United, Ethiopia can grow yet still preserve its unique identity.

Traditions

By Mahfoudh Kayanda

ENSL 0095: Argument

In my country, people are very friendly. They live together like family by helping each other whenever it is needed. Almost everyone in the neighborhood knows one another. When people wake up in the morning, they check on their closest neighbors to make sure that they are okay before they begin their daily routine (i.e. work or school). I think that traditions such as this should be continued and maintained.

One of the benefits of people checking up on one another on a regular basis is that it creates love between neighbors. Someone could've gotten robbed, become sick, died, or maybe just didn't have any food for the day. A neighbor looking out for another neighbor in these and other types of situations could be a major lifesaver. People really feel cared about and are able to get through rough times much better with others helping to keep an eye on them. For example, when my father passed away, my mother didn't know what to do. She was a twenty-nine-year-old with seven children. She was in complete shock at the news of my father's death. She had no idea about what her next move should be. It was our neighbors who helped us get through that difficult time. This was mainly due to our good relationship with them.

My tradition of keeping in touch and checking up on my neighbors regularly has helped me even outside of Zanzibar. In January 1998, at Emory University, I had an accident. I bumped my head with another player during a game of basketball. I had no relatives here in the United States except my neighbors. Some of my neighbors came to the hospital where I was hospitalized and took care of me. They paid my rent and other bills for that month because I had to be on sick leave from work for three weeks. I believe that the reaction of my neighbors to my condition was mainly related to my carrying on a tradition of showing concern for the neighbors on a daily basis.

In conclusion, I didn't understand why people acted so toward their neighbors. However, once I had some difficulties, I truly understood (in a major way) the benefit of being close to one's neighbors. I was reminded once more of how it was our neighbors who helped me and my family out at the time of my father's death. They also helped us out under countless other circumstances. I realize today that it is always good and helpful to have friendly and concerned neighbors.

Essay on a Social Issue: Legalization of Marijuana

By Cem Ultav
ENSL 0081: In-class essay, argument

Marijuana is a kind of weed that grows in the hot places of the world. Marijuana is a very common weed in the world. Marijuana smokers say that they feel relaxed and happy when they smoke marijuana. Many people in the world believe that marijuana should be legal. I also believe that marijuana should be legal. I believe it has to be legal because it does not have such bad effects as people think. It makes people feel better, and it has to be legal because of allowing the drinking of alcohol and the smoking of cigarettes in this country.

Here in the U.S., drinking alcohol and getting drunk is allowed any time unless people drive. Also, smoking cigarettes is allowed anywhere except in public buildings. People can do both of them, but smoking marijuana is not allowed in this country. This means that I can roll plant A and smoke it legally, but if I roll plant B and smoke it, I go to jail for it. It does not sound logical to me. I think the only reason why it is illegal is not taxing marijuana in this country.

Every year a lot of people die because of legal cigarettes. Also, a lot of people go to rehabilitation facilities for addiction to alcohol. People think that marijuana has worse effects on the human body than drinking alcohol and smoking cigarettes. I think this is not true. Marijuana never causes lung cancer. In addition, you do not see anybody going to the hospital because of getting addicted to marijuana. The only bad effect of marijuana on the human body is the killing of brain cells, just like alcohol does.

Marijuana smokers say that they feel better when they smoke marijuana. They say they feel relaxed and happy. In some countries, the doctors prescribe marijuana to people who have high aggression. Marijuana is prescribed by some doctors because it does not have any bad effects on the human body and makes people feel better.

Those are the reasons why I believe that marijuana has to be legal. Some people want to smoke it, and it is not a drug. It makes some people feel better, and it has less bad effects than smoking legal cigarettes and drinking legal alcohol. I believe that smoking marijuana has to be legal in every place in the world where there is freedom.

Topic: "The willingness to marry without love is also subject to cultural variation." Discuss the relative advantages and disadvantages of arranged marriages.

Marriage in Albania is one of the most important and central ceremonial moments in a series of national rites and rituals connected with a person's life. Not more than forty years ago in the highlands of Albania, "being married in the cradle" was a common expression. People used to get "married" long before they started thinking of it, and it worked!

The Albanian wedding ritual has been preserved in its entirety as a series of festivities rich with elements of folk-drama. These festivities consist of a pre-marriage, marriage, and after-marriage rites and rituals. Pre-marriage is the period when the two families are being introduced and acquainted, while "The Boy" and "The Girl" are not supposed to know each other. This is a continuous process, and it used to start when the two families decided to marry their newborns. The most surprising tradition is that the groom was not supposed to see the face of the bride until the very last moment, when they officially got married. In regards to this type of marriage, on the one hand, love is not a primary issue. But, on the other, respect is the material and curiosity to discover each other is the builder of the marriage. This is what made those marriages work at first, and after, maybe even love, love for the family, for each other (as a result of the mere exposure effect), and for their children.

From another viewpoint, the modern marriage has a different developing strategy. The ones who make the choices are the main protagonists, most frequently a girl and a boy. They decide whom to love, how to love each other, and when to get married. Before they get married, they know, discover, explore, and, in the end, love each other. This is an interesting part of our life, getting into and being part of someone else's life most intimately. The increasing power of feelings, love, compassion, and attraction, which grows as the time passes, makes our lives happier and healthier until a certain moment when all this stops and starts decreasing. Love sometimes can be like a flying pebble; when you throw it, it goes high in the sky, but soon after that, it starts falling, and you do not know where it is going to land!

If I compare these two ways of getting married, theoretically I think that the first one, the arranged marriage, is the best. I think that being curious and then discovering and loving somebody you don't know is an interesting but not an easy "job" to do. However, as a hard job, it has a valuable reward: "new love while not being young." Practically, though, I think that I have to experiment with my own feelings and emotions to find my missing part, which maybe I found! After all, this is my life, and it has to be my choice whom to get married to.

Marriage will be the greatest experiment of my life, and I hope it will work out the first time. Madame Virginie de Rieux, a 16th-century French writer, wrote: "Marriage is a lottery in which men stake their liberty and women their happiness." Let's hope I won't lose a lot.

Practice ESL Regents' Essay

By Simone Mendez

RGTE 0199

Topic: What, in your opinion, are some of the reasons why so many people have pets?

I wish I were half the person my dog thinks I am. There is so much love and acceptance in those devoted eyes! The feeling I get from looking into his eyes alone would be reason enough for me to have a pet. However, most people choose to share their lives with a pet for the safety, for the health benefits, and for the companionship a pet can provide.

Perceptive pet owners may use the change in their pets' behavior to their advantage. Pets, in particular dogs and cats, have an acute sense of hearing and smell. These acute senses, in addition to the pets' inherent animal instinct, make them react immediately to any changes in their surroundings. If they feel a disturbance to their environment, such as the presence of fumes generated by a gas leak or a fire, or the sounds of an intruder, their behavior will change noticeably. They may be agitated and nervous or be unusually quiet and hide. So, regardless of their size, pets are excellent alarms. As a result, pet owners can feel safe, which is almost as important as actually being safe.

Not only may having pets save one's life one day, but having pets may also improve the quality of one's life healthwise. Studies continue to unveil the great effects that having pets have on one's health. Among these benefits, a few are worth mentioning: for instance, people who have regular contact with pets have lower blood pressure and are less susceptible to stress. In addition to that, people who own pets are less likely to suffer from minor depression. Moreover, those who suffer from acute depression episodes report that after getting a pet the episodes were further apart and shorter in duration. Some of these health benefits derive from the catharsis that having a pet may provoke, as pets are primarily companions.

Companionship is another reason why people have pets. The companionship shared with a pet is usually of a deeper level than the one human beings share among themselves because people project their own personalities onto their pets. Thus, people tend to see in their pets' eyes exactly what they need to see, whether it's love or sympathy, acceptance, or playfulness. Pets provide a welcome relief from the self-critic that lives inside of us. And while the voice inside of us may be harsh and sometimes put us down, the interaction with our pets is usually uplifting. Pets can be good companions to people of all ages. Children benefit from the responsibility of caring for pets as much as from enjoying them as playmates. Adults may rely on their pets for comic relief at the end of the day. Elderly people find that caring for pets may be a hobby. In any case, provided pets and owners are compatible, pets make excellent companions.

In summary, the major reasons why people choose to have pets are for the safety, the health benefits, and the companionship pets provide. People who have pets feel safer at home, as they can rely on their pets to be good alarms. In addition to that, life with pets may lower blood pressure and lessen the effects of depression. Furthermore, pets make good companions. So, life with pets is overall richer and happier. And that's the bottom line. That's why people have pets. Here, boy!

A Confused Mind: An Analysis of Judith Guest's *Ordinary People*

By Sergio Gill
ENSL 0090: Literary Analysis

Conrad Jarrett, a seventeen-year-old adolescent, is one of the most important characters in the novel *Ordinary People* by Judith Guest. After a suicide attempt and spending eight months in a mental institution, he returns home trying to deal with many problems and hardships that everyday life brings him. A traumatic accident in his childhood, in which his brother dies, causes him pain, depression, and guilt.   Also, new experiences in his everyday life create interesting questions about illusion and reality, presented from an appealing and abstract point of view in Conrad's mind. Now he has to get answers to so many questions.

At the beginning of the novel, Conrad thinks about a "search for identity." He says that everyone needs to reach for a destination, arrive at an opinion about something, and adhere to a guiding principle for the rest of his or her life. He refers to it through a really comical example, the bumper sticker. On the highways, all the cars are giving messages about everyone's beliefs, and all recapitulate their convictions in a few words: "Be Kind to Animals—Kiss a Beaver"; "I Have a Dream, Too--Law and Order"; "Jesus Saves at Chicago Fed"; "Honk If You Love Jesus"; "Rod McKuen for President" (1). Vaguely, he remembers his old personality. He used to have a good sense of humor, quite a contrast with a depressed person who only thinks about failure and anxiety. *"Life Is a God-Damn Serious Big Deal*—he should have that printed up to put on his bumper [. . .]" (2).

He usually thinks too much, a bad thing after living in a mental institution. He wants his life to be as it used to be. In his room the only things left are the colors and the shadows on the

17

wall: pale blue and gray. "Pale blue. An anxious color. Anxiety is blue; failure, gray. He knows those shades" (1-2). That is actually a really interesting thought. Colors make a great impact in our life. In a movie, painting, or any art statement, the colors propose feeling, performing the main point of the manifestation. In many ways, certain occasions are represented by colors.

But what is really in his mind about existence? Is life a true statement about reality? What is in his inner self? He tries hard to forget about everything and be just like other "ordinary people." But how hard is it for him to be "normal"? One of Conrad's dreams may bring the answer about reality and fantasy in his life:

> *Brightness surrounds him. No shadows but it must be night [. . .] . He walks. The moon is above him and to his left [. . .] the mouth of the tunnel appears a metal cylinder curving ten feet over his head, the lower rim buried in the sand. (76)*

Somehow we know it is about suicide. That claims our attention and reminds us all about the "Razor-blade" experience: *"A sharp right-turn ahead obscures his view when he turns the corner there is disappointment [. . .]"* (76). Conrad is connecting his life with the dream; he thought life would be interesting. But later he found out that life is not what he was expecting: *"He stands discovering that the dimensions have shrunk again [. . .]"* (76). That is a feeling of entrapment, which he tries to escape. But it is too late; he tries to follow a way out, but the disappointment of being in the wrong place is too painful. He wants to give up. It is hard for him to find peace. Untouchable reality claims every day as he looks for answers. He perceives tranquility. The dream replays the sounds of the ocean, then nothing but silence. There is no place to go. Life did not give any opportunities. *"He is convulsed with panic begins to work himself backward [. . .]"* (77). He cannot breathe. He screams. The violence takes place in the dream.

At the end, when everything seems to be perfect, Karen's death is a shock that breaks everyone's heart. This is a critical point in the novel: *"So safe so safe floating in the calmest of seas what happened?"* (212). He remembers good times with her, laughing and having fun, "[. . .]*Karen's legs swinging back and forth back and forth and the blue cotton dress clings to her slim body* [. . .]" (212). He talks about the color again, "Pale blue, anxious color." He does not want to think about it; it's really painful and uncontrollable. He wants to sleep.

Conrad relates certain feelings with colors again and again. "*Shock. His mind egg-shaped gray loose tracing of paths* [. . .]" (212). Another example is "[b]lue bedspread, blue-and-white-striped wallpaper, blue-and-white rag rug on the floor" (213). Karen's dress in the dream is "blue cotton" (212); the walls "have been freshly painted. Pale blue. An anxious color. Anxiety is blue; failure is gray" (1-2). For Conrad's life, everything still is as usual, the same house, the same neighborhood, the same friends. But he is more secure now. He established his "search for identity" in one way or another. Life by itself provides enough experiences for everyone in order to grow up.

Work Cited

Guest, Judith. Ordinary People. NY: Penguin Books, 1976.

On June 7, 1997, I went to the middle part of Thailand to a place called Rayong. Many people told me that there is a beautiful and elegant island there. The more that people persuaded me to visit that island, the more I craved to go. Finally, when my desire reached its peak, I grabbed my baggy old blue jeans, my yellow, pink and blue tie-dyed shirts, my lingerie, toothbrush, toothpaste, and my favorite flip flops with a white flower on top and stuffed them all in one bag. I caught a tour bus at ten o'clock in the morning, and I sat in the back row on a badly worn leather seat. Along the way, I smelled smoked chicken coming through the window from an old rusty tin cart outside the tour bus. Suddenly, I turned to my left, hearing the wood seat creaking, and I saw an old lady in her sixties sitting down next to me. She gave me a big smile, and with great astonishment, I saw my reflection from her golden teeth. We carried on an interesting and animated conversation during our journey. She told me an interesting story about an island in Rayong. She said that a long time ago there was an infant elephant that got lost from his mother. At night the restless sailors in the deep blue sea would hear mournful sounds of an elephant crying. Before long, the elephant lay down and died in the middle of the lonely sea because of his depression from missing his mother. Over time, trees began to grow from him, and he became a famous elephant known as the "Elephant Island."

When the bus reached Rayong, I thanked my companion for telling me her exotic story about the island. After I left the bus, I took a ride on a small engine boat to the island I'd been long waiting to see. Ahead of me I could see a small green dot in the middle of the ocean that slowly grew up into a humongous green island in the shape of an elephant. After the boat docked and I went ashore, my feet sank into the powdery white sand. I knew that my visit to this place would become a most favorite memory of mine.

I wandered around and gazed in amazement at the island that many people had told me about. Facing towards the sea with my eyes closed, I could feel the cool, gentle breeze of the wind touching the tip of my nose, echoing through my ears, and stretching my long black hair up into the sky, like feathers blown up into the weightless air. Opening my eyes, I saw an aqua-blue sea that reflected the sun's rays, causing billions of white sparkles beyond the surface, like gallons of diamonds that had been dumped into the sea. I turned backwards and saw the gigantic elephant island that was sleeping sideways, bending in a "U" shape towards me, as if it was going to wrap me into a California Roll. On my left and right there were palm trees that extended into the horizon. In a moment, I heard the deep sounds of ships' horns as they approached the shore. Once again I faced to the sea, and big white foams of waves were rolling madly in my direction, creating a spray that covered me. I laughed and licked my lips, tasting the salt of the sea. The taste of the salt on my dry lips made me realize that I was thirsty, so I decided to walk to the resort nearby and get a glass of water. Since I decided that I was going to spend the night at the resort, I then asked the clerk if they had an air-conditioned room. They were unavailable, so I had to sleep in a small hut.

As I walked toward the hut, the sand forced me to drag my legs and my bags. Finally, the hut appeared before me; the location of it was perfect because it was right on the shore. It was made out of bamboo, and the roof was made out of dry palm tree leaves. Also, it was lifted up from the ground and had an extended platform where I sat and enjoyed the scenery. The window was very unique, like a dog door. When I went to open the window, I had to use a stick to prop it open. Inside the hut there was only one bed with a mosquito net and a lantern. The door had no lock, so when the sun went down and the moon rose, I was so frightened that someone was going to come in and attack me. I solved the problem by stretching my long legs against the door, being prepared to kick anyone attempting to enter. Finally, the soothing sounds of the waves lulled me to sleep.

After several wonderful days on the island, my last day arrived. On my last day, I walked into the forest without any particular destination in mind. Looking through the trunks of trees that poked up from the rich soil in great profusion, I could see beams of light filtering through the forest. With curiosity, I followed the light, and when my journey ended, I was delighted with the vision of rows of beautiful white rocks that curved around the island. Without hesitation, I climbed the rocks one by one as if I were climbing giant stairs. I was searching for a rock that would give me the greatest view. Once there, I saw the big blue sea and the sky as if they were combined together as one, with little white seagulls soaring through the unlimited space, like shooting stars dropping down to the sea. At that point I felt I was the luckiest person on earth.

This journey was important to me because it made me realize that great wealth and modern conveniences are not the things that make me happy. It is the joy and wonder of the simple life close to nature. At the end of my stay, I realized that my experience on the island had fully lived up to my initial expectations.

The Love I Have for Classical Music

By Erreka Kenyarda Reed

English 0099: Practice Exit Essay

One stressed afternoon, the Overton High School Chamber Choir, the most advanced choir out of the seven, was rehearsing for the spring concert that goes on every year. It was three days away, and everyone was getting excited about performing the wonderful pieces that we had been rehearsing for one month. The concert was going to be held in the school auditorium at night. This was my second year being a part of this choir with Lulah Hedgeman, the best choir teacher in Memphis, TN. As we were rehearsing one of the pieces, "Lament for a Lost Child" by Jere Hutcheson, I began to imagine what the composer was thinking about when he wrote this piece. The piece was based upon sounds and gestures often performed spontaneously by children. The composer attempted to use these activities in such a way as to express memories of a lost child. The composer also intended the audience to imagine the whole scene by listening. Classical music is all about listening and imagining. I became fascinated by how different composers come up with ways to get people to listen to their music. From that moment of singing that piece, I was eager to learn and experience more about classical music. That is why I prefer listening to classical music, because it helps me to enjoy performing, it is a stress reliever when I'm at my weakest point, and it has a lot of history that makes me eager to learn more about what I enjoy—music.

I enjoy performing classical music because it allows people to see the gift that God has given me. I have always been misjudged. I used to sing in talent shows, singing R&B and gospel tunes. Everyone thought that was the only style I knew how to do. When I attended Overton High, I was always willing to perform a

23

classical piece, but I would never get a chance to do it because I accepted my reputation. Someone once told me that I had a gospel voice, and I didn't stand a chance of singing classical music. I took that as a motivation. My choir teacher, Lula Hedgeman, told me that I was blessed with a voice, and I had the ability to sing any style I wanted to sing. She made me sing a solo at our first concert my junior year, and I began to see that classical music is what I want to perform. When I was at DePauw, I got a chance to be in an opera, "Dido and Aeneas," by Purcell. I also got a chance to audition for this college in Vienna as an intern. I received $10,000 to attend for a semester before I graduate. I wanted to challenge myself because I was scared that my voice was going to be taken away. My mother told me when I was fifteen that if I didn't use my talent, that God was going to take it away. I was determined to use my voice to the best ability I had, and that's how I became active in classical music.

Another reason why I enjoy listening to classical music is that it relieves stress when I'm at my weakest point. When I was at DePauw, I was stressed over academics, and the only thing that kept me going was music. When I would attend voice class, I would be so relieved from singing. Vergene Miller, my voice teacher, would make me cry before I sang because I would always come to voice lesson crying. I would feel so much better when she would tell me to imagine the person while singing. I would change my whole character. By the end of different pieces like "Porgi, amor" by Le Nozze Di Figaro or "Cassandra's Lullaby" by Mark Fax, I would forget the problems I had before going to the lesson. Sometimes I would listen to classical pieces in my room and meditate. My favorite pieces that I often listen to are "Piano Sonata in C minor, Op. 13 (Panthetique), Second Movement," by Beethoven; "Erkling, D," by Schubert; and "Water Music, Suite in D minor," by Handel. I would feel so relaxed because the music would be touching and full of warmth. I found that to be easier to listen to.

The history of classical music is known throughout the country, but it's not a typical style of music that people would prefer often. Classical music has a lot of history behind it, so I always look forward to learning more of it. At voice lesson I would get introduced to a new song, and my voice teacher would have me go to the library and look up the composer, singer, and history of the piece. That would allow me to learn the piece faster and perform it better. I would know what I'm singing about. The first semester at DePauw, I took a history class that was very interesting. My teacher would have the class listen to a recording like "Die Walkure, Act III, Finale" by Wagner and talk about its function and analyze the song. During the quizzes, we would have to listen to a song and write the composer and the date the song was written. I found that it was easier to listen to the music than to someone giving a lecture on different composers. I was actually learning music, and I wanted to explore more of it.

The day of the concert, I was excited about performing, although we had practiced for three days straight. My teacher gave us a lecture before the performance. She told us to imagine every piece and put ourselves in the composer's shoes. After the wonderful performance, I was eager to perform more, to use it as a stress reliever, and to learn more about the history of classical music.

Music Senses

By Terri-Ann Lee

English 0099: Practice Exit Essay

I was sitting in my room getting ready for bed the other night, and for some reason I was agitated. I then found the reason my nerves were so on edge. The rap music that was playing was the culprit that was making me so agitated. I immediately started flipping the stations until I got to the station I wanted, Peach 94.9, the home of Soft Rock. My nerves were soothed in a matter of minutes, and I was able to relax. I love listening to Soft Rock because it relaxes me, gives me sweet dreams, and clears my head.

Soft Rock is the only kind of music that relaxes me. Every other music, from rap to country, gets on my nerves very badly. For example, I was in my car driving down Memorial Drive last night, and the obnoxious Snoop Doggy Dog and his loud, obscure music came out of the radio. I really wanted to jump out of the window. Snoop's nonsense music never made sense to me, so I changed the station to something more suitable, and I immediately relaxed when Celine Dion's "Where Does My Heart Beat Now" came on. Soft Rock also relaxed me when I got into a fight with my sister, and my mother blamed me for the argument. I was extremely angry, but all I did was turn on my Soft Rock music, and all my anger washed away on the soothing music.

The second reason why I love Soft Rock is because of the sweet dreams it gives me. For example, last night I went to my bed at about 10:00 p.m. I was extremely tired, and my sister had previously been in my room, so I knew the radio was on some rap music station. I was so tired that I couldn't even change the station, and I fell asleep to C-Murder's "f. . . them other . . . ."

Well, the next thing I knew, I was having nightmares about pit bulls ripping me apart and pulling me limb from limb. I woke up in a cold sweat, terrified and shaken. I immediately changed to my trustworthy station, and I fell asleep to sweet, soft music by Mariah Carey. I had a dream that I was sailing on a calm, crystal-clear ocean with dolphins swimming by my boat. The love of my life was also by my side. That is the kind of dream I like.

The third reason why I like Soft Rock is that it gives me a clear head to think. When I listen to rap, alternative, or country music, my head gets all kinds of crazy thoughts, and I can never concentrate on anything. I tried listening to Shania Twain's "Man, I Feel Like a Woman" while I did my homework last Monday, and all I could think about was dancing. Then I changed the station to Toni Braxton's "Why Did You Marry Him," and I started dancing to that also. I then went back to my station, Peach 94.9, and Michael Bolton put me back on the studying train.

I can't help it. Soft Rock is what I love. I like other music, too, but I can only tolerate so much of those other kinds of music. Soft Rock is the only kind of music that I can listen to through the whole day without changing channels. No other music can relax me, give me nice dreams, and clear my head. I would not change my choice of music for anything.

English 0099 Exit Exam Essay

By Meily Poon

Topic: Reasons why students drop out of high school

Every year students are dropping out of high school. In today's society, students do not appreciate school as much as they did forty years ago. Some reasons why students are dropping out of high school are drugs and alcohol, peer pressure, and pregnancy.

Today, there are more people using and abusing drugs and alcohol. Teenagers make up a big percentage of these people. Most of the teenagers that drink or do drugs cause their grades to drop gradually, making them want to drop out of school. Most of these drug-using "dropouts" end up working at the local fast food restaurant to support their bad habit. The dropouts usually do not have a future to look forward to because they will either overdose on drugs or alcohol or let their habit run their lives.

Another reason why students drop out is because of peer pressure. Many people are gullible and naïve. They let their friends persuade them into doing anything just so they can be cool or fit in. Peer pressure can also be associated with being in a gang. Students who are in gangs usually end up dropping out because most of them feel that school is a waste of time. They become "brainwashed" by their fellow gang members or friends into believing that school is for "nerds" or that school is not cool. Most of these high school dropouts end up either on the streets, in jail, or dead, but some of them may be lucky and get a minimum-wage job instead of dying.

The last reason is teenage pregnancy. Teenage pregnancy has been a major problem for decades, and the problem is finally getting a little better, but for the ones who are still getting pregnant in school, they have no choice but to drop out. Every year a child is born to a teenage mother, and in that same year the mother drops out of high school. Most of the mothers never return to high school to graduate, making it hard for them to achieve success in the future. They end up working two jobs because most of the babies' fathers do not take responsibility for their actions. Some single teenage mothers receive support from their mothers so that they are able to graduate from high school, but the ones that do return either drop out again because of their baby or because they feel the school work is too much. The "teenage mother cycle" usually goes from one generation to the next. The teenage mother's child has a high risk of also dropping out and either getting pregnant or getting someone pregnant.

Education is very important, especially in today's society because of all the new technology and fields, but students are still dropping out because of these reasons. Students need to stop dropping out, because if they do not, then our next millenium will not occur.

English 0099 Exit Exam Essay

By Kali Williams

Topic: Reasons to obtain a college education

I have always felt the need to go to college. I always thought that it was important because I saw my parents struggle for a few years out of my life. I have always wanted to be someone and make a difference in people's lives. My parents would tell me that the best way to make a difference is to further my education. The reasons why I feel it is important for me to obtain a college education are that I will feel better about myself, and I will be able to get a job that will help me make a difference.

It is important to me that I finish college because I know I will feel good about myself. I already feel good about myself just knowing that I am in college. Receiving a diploma and knowing that I have made my way through elementary, middle school, high school, and college will make me feel good. I also know that I will make my family proud of me, which always makes me feel good. Knowing that I have achieved something in life is important to me. I know that I didn't go through thirteen years of school just to stop after a high school diploma. I am determined to make a difference.

The other reason why obtaining a college education is important to me is that I can get a better job with a college diploma. I am going for my nursing degree because I like to take care of people who I know need someone to be there for them. Being a nurse is a good-paying job, but I'm not doing it just for the money. When I was in high school, I became a certified nursing assistant. In order to get the certificate, I had to actually work in a nursing home and a hospital. While working in the nursing home and hospital, I saw how important it was to those patients that we take care of them. Knowing that I was needed made me want to help them all the time and in any way possible. With a college education and a nursing degree, I will be able to do what I love most, helping people.

In conclusion, a college education is very important to me. It will make me feel good about myself and get me the job I love most, nursing. I have a strong determination to finish school and be someone. I truly want to help those less fortunate. With the determination I have, no one can stop me from being what I want to be.

Moving Away From Home

By Shelicia Reese

English 1101: In-class essay, narration

Moving away from home was a demanding yet learning experience for me. I believe the thought has sporadically crossed nearly every teenager's mind. Of course, it may seem like the best thing to do at one point. Our young minds are only thinking about the freedom, privacy, and even having that "grown-up" feeling. After I had actually taken that big step that I thought would be easy, reality gradually unfolded. Everything my parents had warned me about before, like expenses and responsibilities, had become actuality; even unknown feelings began to evolve. I began to feel ways I never expected to feel at my age.

I was an eighteen-year-old freshman in college when I felt the need to move out. I was working for a major phone company, making enough money to pay my parents' mortgage each month. Every pay period I would wonder just what I could do with all the money I was saving. I wasn't paying a car note on the car I had, so none of it went to that; even after giving my parents money bi-weekly, I would still have a large amount left over. One day after an argument with my parents about my spending a huge amount of money on clothes, the suggestion that I move out came up. My parents were in complete awe that their "little girl" was thinking about moving away. They said a lot of things trying to convince me that I was about to make a huge mistake. But that didn't stop me; actually, it made me want to do it that much more.

I moved out at the beginning of the summer. I had found a nice apartment near the campus, which seemed to be the size of my parents' living room, paying $545 monthly. After paying security deposits and first-time fees, I had nearly cleaned out what I had saved. Slowly, expenses seemed to be coming from every direction. It had been not even a month when I came home to my apartment to find a huge stack of mail in my box. I thought that maybe it was mail for the tenants who had lived there before me. Looking through the crisp envelopes, I saw my name printed in each of the windows: BellSouth, GA Power, and Atlanta Gas Light bills. I threw them on my small bed that I had bought from a local furniture store and neglected to open any of them.

Two months had passed since I had moved out of my parents' home. Classes would be starting soon. I had paid the $545 rent for a second time and bought myself a nice two-piece set for my living room. I thought everything was going smoothly until I received three pieces of mail with "past due" stamped across the front of them. That's when I remembered the bills that I never opened and looked at. In between buying books for the four classes I was registered in (about $150 a piece), paying rent and eating take-out food every night, my bills slipped my mind. By this time, I was working overtime at my job to be sure I could pay for the piles of bills and continue to buy food, pay rent and any school costs, and put gas in my car.

Secondly, on top of all the costs I was stuck with, I had almost four times the responsibilities I had when I was at home with my parents. I had to be sure to make it to my full-time job and classes every day, and I had what seemed like daily deadlines I would have to meet to either pay bills, complete assignments or present projects. I also had to make decisions such as staying after school for tutoring or going to work instead to make every cent I could earn. Because I made decisions that I felt were necessary, my grades began to weaken. I was eighteen years old, and I felt like I was being forced into the world. But I realized that I had decided not to listen to my parents and had instead chosen to move out.

Lastly, moving away from home made me feel ways I never thought I would feel. On days when I had tests, I would worry about what the grade would be because I had spent nearly the entire night before working to pay living expenses. There were nights when I would lie in my bed and imagine my brother barging in my room asking for a CD. There were times when I longed for the late-night woes of my little sister. I never thought that leaving home would make me experience these different emotions. But I was also full of pride—that would not let me go back home or ask my parents for anything. I left when they tried to stop me, so I decided I would have to do it all myself.

To conclude, many teenagers go through a phase when they have the exact opposite thoughts of their parents. Because of this, they feel the need to move out. Leaving home at an early age was a major step for me, and it wasn't easy. I basically coerced myself into being an adult by paying costs, taking responsibility for making wise decisions, and even dealing with feelings I didn't expect to deal with. Everything my parents had told me I would encounter as a result of moving out happened before I knew it. But I did learn the facts of life during my experience. If I could do it all over again, I would definitely do it differently.

The Danger of a Frozen Bagel

By Mike Randazzo

English 1101: Narration

"Oh, dude, that really hurts."--attributed to the author, exactly one second after the finger-slicing incident.

It's a funny thing the way embarrassing stories seem to have so much more longevity than the heroic ones. You rescue a hundred babies from a burning building, and people forget the next day. But make some stupid mistake, and it follows you like a social assassin for the next five years, the story retold whenever the same so-called friends are around to badger you. About three days ago, I was at a bar with one of my old college roommates and a couple of friends when we started reminiscing about our old dorm room. We talked about everything--the good, the bad, and the disgusting. Jesse, my old roommate, decided that, for the umpteenth time, he would like to tell the story of how I managed to nearly sever my right index finger while slicing a bagel with a table knife.

I was nervous enough to begin with my freshman year of college. The school was exponentially bigger than my high school with several thousand more students who all seemed to know more about what was going on than I did. Orientation was spent wandering around like a confused sheep, getting lost, not remembering my classes, and experiencing several other academic woes. It was during this time that I got to meet my three dorm roommates--Jesse, John, and Sean--and become acclimated to the college realities of no parents, no parents, and, well,. . . no parents. My excitement increased after finding out that my roommates

35

shared the same party aesthetics as I did, and we set out at once to declare ourselves extremely inebriated.

During the course of this week, with little or no movement whatsoever, we managed to enter a purple haze Hendrix would've been jealous of, sleeping until two or three in the afternoon, and going to bed around five or six in the morning. Yes. . . sweet paradise, this was the seven-day stretch before classes began, a mind-numbing descent into the furthest reaches of pre-academia dementia.

On the seventh day, let it be said that I rested. And the resting was good. Unfortunately, it was not enough time to escape the surly chemical tentacles which had held me so tightly for the past week, refusing to let go even the next morning, the first dreaded day of classes.

I woke up a little late, around 7:15 a.m., to find my three roommates preparing breakfast, making jokes, and getting ready for our first class, Drawing 112, which began at eight. We had managed to build up a little group of friends during the last week, and a couple of them showed up that morning to walk to class together. Soon the powerful smell of breakfast overcame me, and I decided it might do some good to eat a nice bagel, toasted and covered with a rich, thick layer of cream cheese. So delicious and haze-clearing was the idea of this bagel, that I failed to notice it was pretty much frozen solid after a week in the freezer, having become more like an inedible piece of steel than a round dough wheel with a hole in the center. Now, I've cut steel, and I've sliced a bagel before, but I've never cut steel with a table knife at 7:35 in the morning dazed out of my mind. I was sawing away, sending crumbs of ice-encrusted bagel flying over the counter like little frozen suicides, too cold to go on with bagel life, when my hand took on a tragic life of its own and slipped from the peak of this pastry pinnacle.

The blood took a second to come, but then there it was, filling up the gash in my hand. Where at first I saw tissue and bone, I now saw the Nile, a great red-river of pain, cascading over

36

the counter and splattering the floor in a violent crimson rain. Jesse was the first to see the trauma before my vocal cords agreed to cooperate with my nerve endings and let out a short moan. He seemed more than eager to point it out to the other five people in the room, who in turn looked my way, some gasping and others muttering expletives in amazement at my bad misfortune.

The first few minutes of pain and panicking I remember very well due to the thousands of synapse-fast reactions and thoughts my brain sent streaming throughout my body. I've heard it said that when someone's body or mind undergoes a trauma, the subconscious will literally erase it from memory. I had no such problem. The pain sent all my senses into overdrive, my vision slowing to a crawl for a second while my brain tried desperately to send directions to my body. I moved, and then I stood still. I opened my mouth and shut my mouth, resulting in more of a stuttering effect than actually fully hinging itself to one extreme or the other. Only after several seconds, with the realization that (a) I was not dying, and (b) my finger was still there, did I have the sense to get a paper towel, apply pressure, and make my way to the resident assistant's room to seek medical attention. Luckily for him, the RA was not in his room, but his roommate *was*, unluckily for him. He opened the door and looked at me expectantly before glancing down at the mess I was holding in my hand. His face turned white at the sight of the paper towel drenched in blood covering my right hand, which appeared to be the source of the aforementioned flow. He told me the RA had already left for class and I should do something else instead. And with that he closed the door, probably vowing never to live with another RA again.

In a bloodletting panic, I realized I had one option left: I decided to call my mom and get her advice. My roommates had already left for the class I was missing while was on hold at my mom's office where she works as a nurse. I recounted as much of my story as I could through short gasps of shuddering air, and she agreed to come pick my sorry self up from the dorms and take me to a hospital.

This was the deepest cut I believe I've ever had, and the doctor was impressed also. After inspecting my poor index finger wound, prying it open with tongs, and giving me a shot, I was informed that a hand specialist would be required to handle this one. The doctor explained to me how when suffering a deep laceration, many main nerves may be severed by the knife, which, in fact, mine were. Through the stitching process and the little joke session the doctors seemed to love, I realized my finger lacked any feeling at all, and it couldn't be solely attributed to the anesthetics. Indeed, it was numb and stayed that way for several years after, feeling more like a dead piece of wood on my hand than a finely tuned feeling instrument. Only recently have I gotten a majority of sense back into it, but sometimes I can tap it and it feels distant, like a shout through a long hall, reverberating slightly through deadened nerve endings.

In classic fashion, sometimes before it rains or when there is some subtle atmospheric change, I can feel a tingling within my finger like tiny pins and needles. To this day, I still harbor little fantasies of myself as an old codger up in the North Georgia woods predicting the weather with my famous numb digit.

Bagels have since been filed into my subconscious as a seemingly innocuous breakfast food with amazingly sinister hidden intentions. I don't think for the rest of that year I craved bagels anymore, and every time somebody was having one, I wanted to issue a warning of the danger lurking just around the corner. In time these fears eventually subsided, and I was able to once again consume my most favorite of breakfast foods, only now I buy the pre-sliced variety and definitely not the frozen kind.

The Kiss

By Vanessa Arcio

English 1101: Narration

I blew a kiss to a skinhead today. I was pumping gas, and he happened to catch my eye as he drove away from his pump. He gave me a look of hatred, and at first I thought that maybe he was an old friend of mine that I had pissed off back in high school, but then I saw the swastika stickers in his car and realized his head was shaved. I looked deep into his eyes, and it was like everything went in slow motion. I studied his look and found disgust. The only thing I could think of to do (besides give him the finger) was to blow him a kiss. So I did. He became infuriated and sped off, leaving tire tracks on the white pavement of the gas station. The noise, as he sped off, was loud and scary. Had I not been fully aware of his action, I would have jumped at the sound. I acted as if the loud noise he made with his car did not affect me, but inside my heart was racing. I wanted him to look back in his rearview mirror and see that he did not affect me with his evil stare and childish attempts to pour fear into my soul. I let the pump reach $8.00 and then put the nozzle back on the gas thing. I paid with my card outside so there was no need to go in and see the Indian owner who, by the way, was also staring at the skinhead as he pumped his gas. I just got in my car and drove away.

I thought for a split second that maybe the skinhead was waiting for me around the corner. I could just see him wearing fitted blue jeans and a black T-shirt with some message on it, hoping to offend someone. I laughed as I thought of him wearing his suspenders pulled up so tight that his jeans hugged in uncomfortable places. Don't get me started on those black boots, laced all the way up his leg with, of course, white shoelaces. I imagined all of this on the way to the airport to pick up my boyfriend.

When my silly thoughts of the skinhead faded away, I was left with the raw emotion of being offended. What gives him the right to look at me in such a hateful manner? I should be able to pump gas in peace without the thought of some jerk giving me attitude because he doesn't like the color of my skin. I can't help all the pigmentation I was born with. There is a small part of me that considers his entire attitude his loss. He will never know all the great things he might have known had he not dismissed me so easily. It is one of my beliefs that people benefit from one another. You can only learn so much from being around people just like you. Had he opened his narrow mind, he might have gained a good friend, or maybe he might have learned something. Perhaps he was having trouble in a chemistry class, and, for all he knew, I could have been a chemistry major.

Maybe he would have seen more than just the little black girl pumping her gas. Had he talked to me he would have known that I am not a little black girl, I am a multicultural young woman full of knowledge and a taste for adventure. Perhaps if he had not labeled me, he would have known that my grandfather was a mechanic for the Tuskegee Airmen or that my father is Filipino and Russian, and my mother is Puerto Rican and African American. Maybe he is having trouble in a Spanish class and looking for someone to help him. Now he will never know.

I was less than a mile away from the airport before I realized that I had spent this entire time being crazy about a stupid incident that could have happened to anyone. Well, anyone who isn't exactly like him, the pure white race. As if anyone is one hundred percent anything. Actually, just being white doesn't fit the bill; you must also be heterosexual. As if being gay is such a crime. If people would just mind their own business and channel all of their energy towards something productive like curing AIDS or solving world hunger, then perhaps we would all be better off.

I drove around the enormous airport parking lot for what seemed to be thirty minutes and finally found parking only one mile away from where I needed to be. I walked into the terminal and found a screen that gave the information I needed: arrival time for Atlanta from Orlando delayed. "Great," I thought. I went to gate A23 and went up to the counter. "Excuse me ma'am, I'm waiting for the flight from Orlando to Atlanta. How long do you think they are going to be?" She looked up from her paperwork and said, "What?"

Just then I realized how much makeup this woman was wearing. She had navy-blue eye shadow from her eyelids to her eyebrows. Her mascara looked like two Venus flytraps clamping together every time she blinked. She didn't have on any blush (and thank God for that), but she did have on lipstick. She had very thin lips, but you would have never known by the way she drew her lip liner on, not on her lips, but like three inches from her lips and then had the nerve to paint on blood red all in between the lines. It was not too short of hideous. It took me a moment before I answered her. I just couldn't believe she thought that was attractive. She spoke again, "What can I do for you, honey?"

" Um , yes ma'am, I was wondering if you knew how late the plane was going to be?"

" Which one?"

" The one from Orlando to Atlanta," I said.

" Oh you're at the wrong gate. The gate you want is G16, down that way a little more."

" Oh, I see. Well thank you."

" No problem. I think that plane is twenty minutes late. They had to stop and get fuel." I walked away thinking, "That's comforting."

I walked down to the other gate and found myself a seat pretty close to the terminal. Ten minutes later I was really bored, so I began looking at all the people passing by. It was sweet to see the little children passing by wheeling along their Winnie-the-Pooh and Barbie suitcases trying to keep up with their parents. One girl with pretty red hair burst into tears as her boyfriend came walking from the terminal with open arms and a big smile.

Then I spotted this weird looking girl. Actually, I thought the uniqueness of her style was cute. She had on baggy jeans like you would see on a teenage boy and a hooded jacket. I think it was black, but she had washed it so often it had faded to gray. Her hair was dyed a subtle red. She kept it super short in the back and had long bangs in the front. She passed by me, anxious to meet someone at the gate. I watched as she met a girl. She ran to hug her, but the girl she hugged seemed out of it. Her face looked like she had just woken up, and her hair was so wacky. She had shaved all of her blond hair off and left like an inch of bangs in the front. I thought for a moment that maybe they were lesbians. The girl with the shaved head had on army pants and a black jacket with patches all over it. I tried to get a glimpse at what the patches said, but I could not make them out. They walked passed me smiling and talking, and then I saw an image that erased the smile from my face. The girl with the shaved head and blond bangs had a tattoo scratched into the back of her neck. It read "SKINHEAD" in capital letters and covered the entire space of her neck. It blew my mind. I mean twice in one day. I would like to think of myself as open-minded. I want to respect the opinion of others, even if I don't agree with them, but this is wrong, and I cannot see it any other way. I am a poster child for everything Skinheads hate. Not only am I the wrong race, but I am mixed with many nationalities. I know that in their eyes I am not pure, and that really bothers me.

I looked up and saw an image I had been waiting to see all week: my boyfriend. I saw him walk from the terminal searching for me, and I let him roam the section with his eyes.

"Hey, Stranger!" I yelled. His big brown eyes found me, and from that came a smile. My heart began to beat wildly in my chest as I ran towards him. He expected me to stop and hug him, but I continued running and I jumped and wrapped my legs around him. " Oh, I missed you so much!" I shouted.

He began leaning towards the left and said, "I'm happy to see you, too, but I can't carry you and these bags." I jumped down and grabbed a bag. "Here, I'll carry that one. Take this one. It's the lightest," he said.

"Thank goodness, because I parked in Egypt."

He laughed and began telling me about his trip. "Orlando was so beautiful, I can't wait to take you there. One night I was walking back to my hotel room and this guy invites me down to the lobby to play poker with him and his friends. I come, which is surprising for me, because you know how anti-social I am."

While walking through the airport, I noticed that people were turning their heads as we passed. They were staring at us, and it wasn't a stare and smile, it was like a stare of wonder and disapproval. I tried to ignore it, but I couldn't, especially not after we passed this one woman. Not only was she glaring at us but also I heard her tell her friend, "That's offensive!" I turned around and looked at her, and that's when Eric noticed I wasn't listening to him.

"Hey what's wrong? Did you know that lady back there?" he asked. When the ladies realized I was on to them, they began to migrate in the other direction.

"Did you hear what that woman said?" I asked, pointing in her direction.

"No. I was talking. Remember?"

"She said we were offensive!"

"Offensive? Are you sure? That doesn't make any sense."

"Sure it does. I'm black and your white."

"First of all, I'm Italian and you're mixed. Secondly, I think you're just being paranoid. Maybe they were talking about your shirt. I mean, you are showing a lot of cleavage today." He smiled. Normally I would have laughed at that, but considering all of the encounters I had experienced, I just wasn't feeling up to it. I grew silent with my thoughts and Eric noticed.

"Why are you so quiet?" he asked.

"You wouldn't understand; plus, it's a long story."

"Maybe I wouldn't understand it like you understand it, but I have my own understanding."

"Whatever, Eric." I rolled my eyes.

"Look, I know people are going to stare, and some people aren't going to like us together, but they don't have to. All that matters is that we like each other. It's our choice to make and not theirs."

"I don't know, Eric. This is really hard on our relationship."

"Every relationship has to overcome obstacles. Nothing you do in life is going to have one hundred percent approval, so just live and be happy no matter what anyone else thinks."

I thought about that all the way home, and I realized that Eric was right. I've never done anything in my life that has received all positive feedback. There is always someone who doesn't agree, so I should just live and be happy. Life is too short to get caught up on the ignorance of other people.

I told Eric about the kiss I blew to the skinhead. He just laughed and said, "That was pretty clever to blow him a kiss. Kill em' with kindness, huh. He probably spent the rest of his afternoon telling all his hateful buddies about the kiss you had the nerve to blow at him. He wastes his time hating and you spend your time loving. That's the way to go if you ask me."

I leaned over and gave him a kiss for his support. "So what happened on your trip?" I asked. He laughed and started from the beginning.

Lessons in the Midst of Sadness

By Courtney Branen

English 1101: Narration

We were sitting in the chapel as the reverend spoke from the pulpit. We were in shock and disbelief over what had happened. The only sounds I heard were my own sobs and those of the people around me. She was fourteen years old, a friend to everyone she came in contact with, and none of us could imagine our lives without her.

Jennifer Dailey was born in 1982 into a loving Christian home. She was a beautiful and vibrant little girl. At a young age, she had been diagnosed with a genetic condition called Cystic Fibrosis. In the years to come, the hospital became a second home to Jennifer. She was admitted several times a year for various check-ups and tests. As she grew older, the condition grew worse, but her spirit never faltered.

I did not meet Jennifer until the fall of my fourth grade year when we both signed up for recreational cheerleading. The first time I met her, I had no clue that anything was wrong with her. She had a spirit and determination unlike most kids our age, and it was not until a year later that I learned about her disease; however, I would not know the seriousness of it for several years.

In the spring of our sixth-grade year, Jennifer played softball for the first time. She is the only person that I have ever played with that always kept a big smile on her face no matter how well or poorly she played. Because of her condition, she was unable physically to be a great player, but that did not stop Jennifer Dailey from trying her hardest. She loved every minute of the games and practices. That year, we also began taking gymnastics classes together. As was the case with softball, she would never be physically able to do a lot of the tricks she would try, but she never gave up.

Her physical limitations and constant coughing were our only reminders that Jennifer was not as healthy as the rest of us. Above all else, Jennifer wanted to be a normal kid. Unlike her friends, Jennifer had to face the reality of her condition every day of her life. We put it in the back of our minds and never really thought about it. I think we all knew that it was very serious, but as middle-schoolers, we were scared by the thought of a life-threatening condition. So we chose not to face what Jennifer faced. I knew that Jennifer would probably not see her thirtieth year, but that was so far in the future, and I never would have imagined that I would lose Jennifer as soon as I did.

In the spring of our eighth-grade year, Jennifer had been in the hospital for longer than usual. We all knew that something was not going the way it was supposed to go, but the eighth graders at Trickum Middle School expected her to come back any day. I had gotten word that she was not doing well, but nothing could have prepared me for her death.

On March 12, 1997, we came to school like usual. As I was walking up the stairwell to the 8th grade hall, I heard nothing. There was complete silence where voices should be heard. When I reached the hallway, my heart dropped and my stomach ached. What I saw told me everything that I needed to know. People stood at every corner crying on each other's shoulders. No words were spoken by anyone to anyone. We all knew that our friend Jennifer Dailey had died. That was the beginning of the hardest week of my life.

It seemed like the whole school showed up for the viewing at the funeral home. I had never seen a dead body before. Jennifer looked so pretty in her pink dress with all of her makeup on. She looked peaceful as if she were only asleep. I kept asking myself, "Why won't she wake up? Why did this have to happen to someone who brought joy to so many?" It just did not seem fair to me. I cried as I looked at her. I cried when I hugged her parents and her little brother. The pain and the loss I felt was almost unbearable, but I know that the loss her family felt was way beyond my comprehension. I kissed her forehead before I left that day. In less than twenty-four hours my friend would be out of reach for the rest of my time on Earth.

The day of the funeral, the chapel was so packed that people were standing or sitting in every last square inch of the room. Several people said some words about Jennifer, and a few songs were played. I sat there thinking that I was in a dream. It felt like I would just wake up and she would be there laughing and talking; oh, how she loved to laugh. She had a great sense of humor. I was going to miss that and her smiles and just talking to her. She was laid in the ground that day, and I was forced to say goodbye.

This was the first encounter with death that I ever had. I knew in my mind that God wanted Jennifer in heaven with Him, but it was and is so hard for my heart to understand. She was special to so many people and is still missed by all of us. This was my first glance into the reality that life does not last forever. We are not guaranteed our next breath, and this realization taught me to live each day as if it were my last and to cherish the friends I have because they are not always going to be here.

The Loss of Yesterday

By Jennifer S. Kauffman

English 1101: Narration

This past August 11th, the sun was shining brightly, birds sang happily, the flowers proudly held their faces toward the sun, filling the air with their essence. All was fine in the world, except for me. It had been a long, tumultuous year that had plagued my soul with increasing depression. I had spent the last few days weeping endlessly. The very core of my soul was shattered, empty, and only getting worse. My mind tormented me with memories of shattered childhood dreams. Over the past year, the unforgiving reality of my brother's murder distressed me with thoughts of wanting and needing to join my brother.

When I awoke on that fateful Friday morning, I had been dreaming of a reunion with my brother, Carl, which provoked memories of our childhood together. Carl played with me and cared for me while Mom worked long hours just to provide our small family with food and shelter. One of my fondest memories of Carl always makes me smile. When I was about a year old, Carl was eating dinner when I ran up to him and demanded, "I wanna bite-bite!" Carl, ever the jokester, asked, "You want what? You wanna butt-bite!" He then lifted me up and bit me on my rear end! Carl laughed hysterically at my squeals from his loving brotherly torture. There were always such games of sibling rivalry played between us.

I enjoyed being the baby of the family as it meant not having to share the limelight with anyone. If I were excluded from anything, I would seek revenge. One rainy afternoon, Mom and Carl were playing the board came called Aggravation, totally ignoring my pleas for an audience. I quietly sneaked up to the table and grabbed a handful of the game marbles as I politely announced, "Tah-tah-too!" which meant "thank you" in my world. I quickly darted off clutching my prize. From those days on, until my brother's mysterious disappearance in 1984, we had joy in our home, a joy too short-lived.

On June 28, 1984, as Mom and I packed for our annual retreat to Florida for the Fourth of July, eighteen-year-old Carl announced that he wanted to stay home to celebrate with his friends. We shared our hugs, love, and good-byes with Carl as we got into the car. Mom told him if he changed his mind he could join us; after all, we went to the same place every year. A week later when we returned home, Carl had disappeared without a trace. This was only the beginning of my nightmares of despair and lost faith that one day he would come home. At the innocent age of seven, I could not accept the death of my brother as an option. I never gave up hope that he would return alive. That hope ended last year in September of 1999.

Carl was murdered on the 3rd of July 1984. Two men in an abandoned house discovered his body ten days later with no identification. After fifteen years, Carl came home on September 27, 1999, and we finally laid him to rest a month later. From that day on, I fell into deep despair. Indeed, my beloved brother had come home, but not the way his baby sister had dreamed, prayed, and believed he would. The disappearance of my brother haunted me daily for fifteen years. The knowledge of his murder tore at the very core of my soul.

An eerie calmness crept over my exhausted soul. I wiped my tears away and accepted death as my only way out. I quickly collected all the sedative medications prescribed to me and filled a glass with water. As I carefully placed them on the kitchen table, I noticed the last picture of my mother, my brother, and me taken in 1984. I sat down, held the picture in my hand, took a deep breath, placed my hands together and prayed for my brother to receive me on the other side. Chills ran through my body. I swallowed the piles of pills. Darkness came over me.

49

Thirty-six hours later I awoke to see my mother sitting beside me and feeling her hand holding mine. With wells of tears filling her eyes, she said, "Jennifer, why didn't you tell me?" A fresh stream of tears flowed down my cheeks. "Mama, I just couldn't bear the pain any longer." I wept. With this, I began to share my "trail of tears" with her. I told her about all my secret pains that festered deep within me for sixteen years.

Finally, we had come together to work through a past both of us had suppressed and denied. It was this suppression that almost took my life. For sixteen long years we didn't speak much about his disappearance or later about his death. Through this experience, I have learned that it is not healthy to restrain and internalize my suffering. Together, we are now working through our pain and huge loss of my beloved brother Carl. For him and my mom, I have chosen life.

My life, up until age nine, basically followed the normal pattern of boyish childhood. I was a typical elementary school student: I did not like school, I had a set group of friends with whom I frequently spent time, and I enjoyed playing sports and running around. Aside from these activities, I was not concerned with very much. In June of 1994, however, my life changed drastically. My brother, Jonathan, who was four year younger than I, was diagnosed with a brain tumor. The chances that he would survive were unlikely. Slowly my parents and I watched as his mental and physical capabilities diminished, as he lost his hair, and as he became excessively obese due to the steroids used to treat the tumor. We braced ourselves for the worst.

My brother and I had a very uncharacteristic sibling relationship; relatives and friends marveled at how well we got along. We used to watch movies and play ball, Nintendo, and other games together. For such a young boy, he was angelic. Unlike his older brother's early days, Jonathan rarely got in trouble or was a nuisance. He as an incredible person, and I loved him immensely. His slow and painful death was very unreal for me. I repressed my feelings and tried fruitlessly to pretend that everything was one big dream.

I remember vividly the day that he died. I was alone with him and his doctor. My parents had left the room moments earlier to discuss funeral arrangements with our rabbi. He lay on his left side, against the wall, facing me. A string of saliva escaped from his half-opened mouth and made its way slowly to the bed on which he was lying. The doctor had told me that when the gauge that measured his respiration fell below sixty, his life was over. It was in the mid-seventies as I became fixated on the bloated image of my dying brother, and a mixture of emotions swirled in my head. I felt anger, fear, depression, and regret all at once. When I finally regained focus, I glanced at the numeric gauge. It read 57. Trying to fight the tears, I mentioned this to the doctor, who was sitting down filling out forms next to me. He immediately went to inform my parents. My five-year-old brother, he told them, had just died. My dad and mom both came into his room for one last glimpse of their son. My dad began to cry. I had never seen him cry before, so at first I didn't know what he was doing, but then he wrapped his arms around me, and we cried together.

Although I never truly realized it at the time, the death of my brother had a profound effect on my emotional development. It didn't show in my grades or activity levels, but my demeanor had changed. My smiles became less frequent and more forced, yet when my fourth grade teacher asked my why I never smiled, I argued with her and said I smiled all the time. I never would admit to myself that I was hurt emotionally, but I was also quick to yell and insult classmates and friends. It was not really until three to four years later that I truly became myself again. At the time soon after Jonathan's death, however, I thought I was just too strong a person to be affected.

Although my brother and I had an extraordinarily loving relationship, after he died all I could think about was the few times we fought. I remembered the times I would not let him play with my friends, when a friend and I acted wildly at his four-year-old birthday party, or when we fought over the use of a bowling ball. A counselor told me it was a natural part of grief to feel guilty, but it took me a long time to replace these memories with those of the good times we had. I saw myself as a poor brother and felt terrible for not taking advantage of the time I had with him. Perhaps in an effort to redeem myself, I begged my parents for another sibling. My sister, Eliana, came one year later. Although not as angelic as Jonathan, she helped to move my focus from death to rejuvenation.

No singular event led to my recuperation. I went to a support group for a while and had occasional talks with my parents, but none of this had a profound effect on me. One outlet I found that did help me, however, was writing. Throughout the years, Jonathan became a common topic in many of my poems, essays, and papers. Written communication then became my main tool for releasing my emotions.

No one ever wants to lose a family member, but, like other hardships, it can have a positive effect on one's outlook and moral development. The ordeal that my parents and I went through, in my opinion, has made us all better people. Petty and superficial problems do not have the same effect on us as they once did. Now, when faced with stress or adversity, we are able to look more at the big picture and put things in perspective.

Many times in school I come across people who, in my opinion, have not experienced significant hardships in their lives and do not put things into perspective as well as I do. I watch my classmates and friends obsess over a poor grade, a name they were called, or some other relatively unimportant occurrence. While I do sympathize with them because I realize that they really are upset about these things that loom large to them, I am grateful that I do not react in the same way. Whenever I feel myself on the verge of becoming stressed or disappointed, I recall the courage of my brother and my family, and I draw strength from those memories. Having experienced a tragedy myself, I am also able to appreciate my life better in comparison to much of the rest of the world where hardship and suffering abound. I am able to step out of my own shoes for a moment and realize that my current problems are not nearly as serious as they may appear, and I know if Jonathan were here today, he would agree with me.

```
Practice Regents' Test Essay

By Elizabeth Duckworth

English 1101H
```

Topic: Do you believe that recycling should be mandatory? Discuss.

Recycling became a major issue to many Americans in the last ten years because of the mounting evidence regarding the effect of the world's waste on the environment. People became aware of the ever-growing ozone, the melting ice glaciers in the Arctic causing oceans to rise, and the startlingly bad quality of the air the world's population breathes every day. These heavily publicized problems were major issues for several years, and many people began to recycle. The trend to take part in the battle to save the planet and its inhabitants has not been as widely discussed in the last few years, and people seem to be forgetting the significance of this crusade to save the future. Recycling has become less popular as people have found that recycling takes time out of their busy lives, that the recycling pick-up is not as reliable as the trash pick-up, or that the destruction of the planet is not happening as rapidly as once believed. People seem to be more concerned with convenience and easing the stress of daily living than protecting tomorrow. People must be made aware of the benefits of recycling, but also, recycling must be made mandatory; otherwise, the world's children will have to pay for the environmental sins of today.

Research has proven that recycling is a successful tool for improving the world's environmental health, and this method of improving the environment can be used on a global scale. Landfills are full of things that people could reuse, but still the world makes new materials to replace the discarded items.

Eventually, these products will simply contribute to the trash that is destroying the earth because someday they too will be thrown away. Even producing these new materials is done at a cost to the environment.

What many people have yet to comprehend is the impact of recycling beyond just keeping trash out of the ground. The world's garbage is not all that can be recycled. Factories have the technology to recycle the pollutants that currently escape from the smokestacks at many company plants. Because this technology is so rarely utilized, many people do not realize that it exists. The new technology is expensive to put into operation, and many companies find it more economical to let their exhaust escape into the atmosphere. Of course, these pollutants add significantly to the problems of global warming, melting glaciers that cause a rise in ocean levels, and degrading the quality of the air as more and more waste is released each day. Companies across the world are causing the air to become even more densely polluted, but today, creating legislation that forces these companies to become environmentally cautious is not common.

Many people argue that the problems of today's economy, peace issues, and education should take priority over environmental issues. What these people do not realize is that if environmental issues are not addressed with vigor now, the earth will cease to support the life that they are trying so hard to improve. Citizens of the world need to save the planet for tomorrow before they worry about improving the life of today. Parents are expected to love their children more than themselves, but parents must realize that the children of the environmental sinners are those who will suffer. If people are not made aware to recycle reusable materials, and companies are not made to find economical, environmentally friendly ways to recycle the pollutants they emit into the air every day, the world will reach eventual self-annihilation.

```
┌─────────────────────────────────────────────┐
│                                               │
│      Practice Regents' Test Essay             │
│                                               │
│          By Adeline Mills                     │
│                                               │
│           English 1101                        │
│                                               │
└─────────────────────────────────────────────┘
```

Topic: Is there any job that you would absolutely refuse to take? Explain.

The calf stared at me with empty brown eyes, its throat slit from ear to ear. It hung upside down by its back legs as the blood gushed from its neck. This was the picture on the front of a pamphlet called "Why Vegan?" It was my second day working at Sevananda, a vegetarian natural foods store, and I had some time on my hands that particular afternoon. The picture, of course, caught my attention, so I decided to open it up. What I saw that day changed my lifestyle completely. That thin little booklet contained shocking statistics and facts as well as disturbingly graphic pictures, from a pile of crushed fluffy chicks to cows with limbs removed lying in a dark, dirty corner of the slaughterhouse. Since that day a little more than a year ago, I knew that I would never take a job in a slaughterhouse because it is unsanitary, I'm vegetarian, and the treatment of the animals is highly unethical.

One reason I would refuse a job at a slaughterhouse is because they are the most unsanitary places I have ever seen. A few years back I saw an expose on the news about a certain slaughterhouse owned by a major meat distributing company. The young female reporter went undercover as an employee and saw many things not meant for the public eye. One picture sticks out in my mind. In a far corner of the slaughterhouse, the workers had made a pile of refuse. As the woman approached it, I could barely make out the contents of the pile in the dimly lit area. To my horror, there were legs, tails, and even a few heads of cows thrown carelessly onto the concrete floor. There was a large puddle of mostly dry blood encircling the pile. When the camera zoomed in for a close up, maggots and flies, among other bugs, had made a home there. I remember quickly leaving the room at that point, completely disgusted by the meat-packing industry as a whole. I thought twice before eating any more beef, and I certainly consumed no more of that brand.

I would not be an employee of a slaughterhouse because I am a vegetarian. Shortly after I started working at Sevananda, I began to hear many strange stories regarding meat. One in particular was an experiment I decided to try with pork. I bought a cheap cut of pork from Kroger, and when I got it home, I unwrapped it and put it in a shallow pan. I already had a little cheap vodka, so I poured it on the meat. I was horrified to see tiny worms squirm out of the pork. They were very thin and short and would be difficult to see if they hadn't been flipping and flopping so erratically. I quickly wrapped the pork up tightly and threw it away, vowing never to eat it again. These tiny parasites are killed when the meat is cooked, but, even so, I would not wish to eat them. I would also not like to handle them or the meat that contains them, which I would have to do if I worked at a slaughterhouse.

The final reason I would refuse to work at a slaughterhouse is obvious, and that is the unethical way in which the animals are handled. My mind returns to the "Why Vegan?" pamphlet at work. It was filled with examples of poorly treated animals, and two in particular struck me. The pamphlet was divided into sections according to type of animals, and sheep came first. The picture I saw in the beginning of the section was very dark and difficult to make out. I could see what appeared to be a bunch of animals lying on the ground. When I read the caption, it explained that what I was looking at was a pit where dead sheep were thrown. However, not all were dead. There was one sheep in the pile that the authors found alive and rescued it. There was a picture on the following page of the sheep after it was cleaned up. It was missing an eye, was very cut up, and only had tufts of fur left. The other picture came from the chicken section. It showed a mangled, obviously dead hen on the floor. She was almost completely flat, and the only parts of her that I could recognize were her face and a foot. This wasn't the worst part, however. By her side, looking very lost and confused, was a fluffy yellow chick which apparently belonged to the dead hen. I know that animals aren't capable of understanding certain situations, but I'm sure that sheep understood that it was lying in a pile of the dead of its own kind. I'm also pretty certain that that chick knew that the hen on the ground was its mother, and there's no doubt that she was badly mangled.

It's very hard for me to understand how anyone can deliberately cause another creature to suffer. The people who work in slaughterhouses face death and suffering every day, and for what purpose? I condone meat eating. To each his own. It isn't the death that disturbs me so much as the way in which it is done. Many of the practices in the meat-packing industry are cruel and unnecessary. However, no matter how the deed is done, I know that I could not go home feeling good about myself if all I had done all day is killed.

Topic: Should college students be required to take Physical Education courses? Why or why not?

College students tend to take the health of their bodies for granted. Often, they are too wrapped up in the web of school life to realize that they are depriving themselves of a healthy lifestyle. However, if colleges require that students take physical education, the unfortunate reality that they are undereducated in this area might make itself clear to them. Not only does P.E. inform college students how to lead a more healthy life through physical activity and proper diet, but it also encourages a more positive outlook on life and provides an escape from the everyday stresses of college.

In order for us to understand how we can lead a healthier lifestyle, we must have some sort of P.E. in our lives. And when would be a better time than in those essential college years? If we educate college students about the importance of exercise and a proper diet as part of their daily routine, then perhaps we will witness fewer cases of students gaining unnecessary weight due to unhealthy habits. I have several friends who went to college and later came home complaining that they had gained so much weight and were unhappy with the way they looked. These friends of mine had never really had any P.E. and therefore rarely exercised and ate mostly junk food. However, I also have a friend who, before going to college, regularly exercised and knew about how to sustain her body and how to maintain a healthy lifestyle. She, unlike my other friends, did not gain any weight. If we educate students now, perhaps they can avoid the dreaded freshman fifteen that my friends who had not had any P.E. experienced.

"You are what you eat" is a phrase that many Americans use. College students who are uneducated in P.E. often turn to junk food as a source of nutrition when, in fact, it does not provide much nutrition at all. Therefore, they tend to feel depressed because they are not very healthy, which can lead to not looking their best. Exercise and proper diet can help to boost a student's self image and outlook on life. Personally, I always feel better when I have exercised and I have eaten sensibly. College students just need someone to lead them in the right direction and to encourage them to improve. If they do, their entire attitude will change for the better.

My friends often call me complaining that they are extremely stressed out about college, perhaps because of their own high academic expectations which too often war with their social entanglements. Exercise is an excellent source of stress relief and an incredible way to forget about the problems of everyday life, to let loose, and to relax. We need to encourage P.E. among college students so that they will recognize that healthy alternatives to relaxing aside from drinking and partying do exist.

College years focus upon learning. If we educate college students about P.E., then we are helping them to lead happier and more productive lives. Requiring that college students take P.E. can only be beneficial.

What Does it Mean to Be German?

By Tatjana E. Krause

English 1101: Definition

The American Heritage Dictionary defines Germany as "a country of north-central Europe bordered on the north by the Baltic and North Sea. Occupied since circa 500 B. C. by Germanic tribes." However, it does not provide the information on what it is like to be German. I am German, and I know what it is like to be German. I was born in Nikolskoe, Russia; my family moved back to Germany when I was ten years old, and I moved to the United States at the age of eighteen. I know what it means and how it feels to be a German among Russians, Germans, and Americans.

I believe that the first and most intense feeling that all Germans share is the feeling of guilt. As a German, you basically are born with the feeling of guilt. You feel guilty because of the two world wars that were started by the Germans; you feel guilty because over six million Jewish people were killed by the Nazi regime. You feel guilty for all those things, even if you were born generations after they occurred. When you are in another country and have a conversation with a citizen there, almost always the subjects of war and war crimes come up; consequently, you feel the constant need to apologize for your country and your ancestors.

At some point you tire of these feelings of guilt because you personally had nothing to do with those two world wars. You killed no one, and you were not responsible for those events and shouldn't be held accountable. A feeling of defiance comes over you, because you realize that other nations have done equally horrible things, but no one points a finger at them. As an example, the Americans almost eradicated the Native Americans and took their land, but only a few expect them to apologize or hold them accountable. Germans, like the French, the Belgians, and the English, just to name a few, have episodes in their history that cause embarrassment.

The other major feeling that defines how Germans feel about themselves is that, as a German, you are not allowed to be proud of your nationality. After the Second World War, the winners of that war successfully destroyed any sense of pride possessed by the Germans as a nation. It is a common and normal thing for Americans to have their flag hanging in front of their houses. However, in Germany, it is considered a disgraceful thing because it supposedly symbolizes that you are a Nazi. The Americans have a song called "God Bless America." A song of German national pride is unimaginable in Germany because it would be considered some kind of a Nazi hymn. Germans don't feel free to show their national pride even in their own country.

Adolf Hitler, who wasn't even German, was an Austrian who overshadowed the whole country. Because of him, his followers, and the NSDAP, we are looked at as a nation of mass killers. One man cannot define a whole country. For example, if Americans were judged by the behavior of Bill Clinton, it would mean that all Americans lie and have extra-marital affairs.

The new generation of Germans refuses to be identified by this madman. We see ourselves as a nation that produced a large number of great philosophers, such as Kant, Shoppenhauer, Liebnitz, and Heidegger. We are also a nation of great writers, including Johan Wolfgang von Goethe, Thomas Mann, and Herman Hesse. German inventors and scientists like Albert Einstein, Ferdinand Zeppelin, Wilhelm Conrad Roentgen, and Heinrich Hertz developed the theory of relativity, the zeppelin, x-rays, radioactive waves, and many other great inventions. We don't define ourselves as a nation that is responsible for a lot of horrible things that happened in the past. We define ourselves as a nation that has contributed enormously to the progress of our global society.

In my eyes the most important thing that defines Germans in recent years is that we are tired of putting our heads down and constantly apologizing. We have begun to stand up for our country, our past, and our culture. Germans are on their way to regaining national pride since we have a lot to be proud of. We have rebuilt our country twice, and today Germany is one of the leading industrial countries in the world, with the highest standard of education. We are saddened by the actions of Adolf Hitler and his followers, but we are proud of ourselves, our country, and our contributions to the world. It fills my heart with joy and pride to know that a German, Albert Einstein, was elected as the man of the century. It symbolizes that, after all, we have finally been recognized for our contributions.

Hip-Hop and R & B:
Not Necessarily Synonymous

By Niki Neptune
English 1101: In-class essay,
Comparison/contrast

Amidst gales of cheers and applause, a young, platinum-haired man, clad in a white "wife-beater" reminiscent of Marlon Brando's earlier "Streetcar" days and shiny metallic pants, steps onto the vibrantly lit stage of the Teen Choice Awards. Taut lips are stretched into a pretentious smile as the young R & B artist recites his thank-you speech for having just won "Best Hip-Hop Artist of the Year." To blissfully ignorant teeny-boppers, nothing seems amiss, but to true hip-hop and R & B aficionados, a dire error has occurred: somehow, an R & B artist took home a hip-hop award. The idea that such a thoughtless mistake could have even taken place makes apparent a lack of communication within the entertainment industry and pop culture. Although they share common musical roots, hip-hop and R & B are two uniquely different genres of music, and their dissimilarities can be seen through their differences in lyrical content, style of delivery, and the definition of the two terms "hip-hop" and "R & B" themselves.

One of the most prominent differences between hip-hop and R & B is reflected through the content of their songs' lyrics. Crooning, soulful voices and desperate pleas of love or heartbreak characterize a typical R & B song; whereas, with hip-hop, lyrical emphasis is placed summarily on money, fast cars, and sexual prowess. A perfect example would be a comparison between the lyrics of the R & B group Boyz II Men and the hip-hop performers The Big Tymers. The Boyz II Men lyrics go as follows:

> Don't have to stay with someone that makes you cry
> You'll end up killing all the love you have inside
> Can't hope to see the sun if you don't open up your
> eyes

Girl, don't let real love pass you by. . . .
The general subject of the Boyz II Men song is love, whereas in The Big Tymers' song "Get Your Roll On," the subject is money; they rap about expensive cars and jewelry, referring to them by trade or brand name ("Benz," "'Vettes," Hummers, Rolex).

Another aspect of the differences in content between these two types of music is the usage of offensive language. Newly mainstream hip-hop artist Shyne released a single called "Bad Boyz," in which the first two lines of the song contain profanity: "Now tell me who wanna f. . . wit' us / Ashes to ashes, dust to dust / I bang--and leave your f. . .in' brains hang, snitches." Shyne's use of profanity is a far cry from R & B artist Mary J. Blidge's intro: "Today you had a visitor, or should I say an old friend. / But wait a minute, that's not how it ends, no." Both of these songs are supposed to be conveying contempt, but they do so in different ways.

Another illustration of the differences between hip-hop and R & B can be seen through the respective artist's style of delivery. R & B artists sing their songs, seemingly invoking the soul in each syllable, whereas hip-hop artists rap their songs using a stylized, prosaic way of speaking. This difference is shown in the comparison between R & B artist Erykah Badu's "Bag Lady" and hip-hop artist Biggie Small's "Juicy." Erykah Badu stretches her voice to the pace of the song: "Baaaag lady, you gon' hurt yo' back / Draggin' all dem baaags like dat. . . ." Hip-hop artist Biggie Smalls, however, delivers his verses by speaking the words to a particular tempo: "It was all a dream / I used to read Word-Up magazine, / Salt 'N Pepa, Heavy D up in the limousine. . . ." Although individual styles may vary from artist to artist within each industry, it's commonly known that R & B artists sing and hip-hop artists rap.

A final illustration of the differences between hip-hop and R & B can be seen through the definition of the terms themselves. The acronym R & B is derived from the phrase "rhythm and blues," which described a particular style of music that can be traced back to the days of The Supremes and The Temptations and even further back to the career of Billie Holiday. R & B artists like Nat King Cole and Gladys Knight pioneered the music industry, setting forth a progression of styles that makes R & B what it is today: a respected and well appreciated expression of emotion familiarized by a mellifluous voice. Hip-hop, a popular form of street poetry, is commonly recognized as having originated in New York. Its pioneers were artists like Run-DMC, Kool Moe D, and LL Cool J. Hip-hop gained its footing on the streets as an underground music form but became mainstream when color barriers were broken and acceptance of a new style of music became popular.

Many hip-hop artists have been known to do a verse or two on an R & B song, and more often than not, an R & B artist will lend his or her vocal stylings to a hip-hop piece, but the two forms of music are still separated by a delineating line. Mistakes such as those that occurred at the Teen Choice Awards have occurred more than once, which leaves the few that know better to wonder, "Will there ever be a clarification?"

College: Eighteen or Forty

By Jo Ann Terrell

English 1101H:
Comparison/Contrast

More traditional and non-traditional students are attending college today than twenty years ago. A large percentage of high school students have decided to attend college long before beginning their high school education. High school students have career guidance centers. Students are able to participate in high school honor, magnet, and Advanced Placement courses. Some colleges offer summer college programs that allow high school students to take college courses for credit, live on campus, and explore academic and career opportunities. Students can find out what college is all about. In addition, a significant number of students today have parents who are college graduates. Students have role models to motivate them to attend college. The higher the students' family income, the more likely they are to attend college. On the other hand, there are non-traditional students, particularly in their forties, who have decided to either return to or begin college. Unlike the traditional college students, they have not had an opportunity to prepare themselves for the fast pace of college life. While attending college can be rewarding for eighteen-year-olds, at the age of forty, it requires extra effort and good planning.

Today, there are many eighteen-year-olds coming straight out of high schools who have decided to attend college. Students who attend college after high school have personal advantages. Many students live at home with their parents rather than on a college campus. Living at home generally causes less stress for students. Students do not have to worry about responsibilities such as rent, food, utilities, and gas. In addition, most eighteen-year-olds are claimed as dependents on their parents' health insurance plan; therefore, they do not pay for health or dental expenses. Their class schedule is more flexible. Students can schedule classes any time during the day or evenings and have extra time to take advantage of extra curricular activities offered at college.

In addition, attending college at eighteen can be monetarily rewarding. Today's students generally work a part-time job. Families today plan and set aside funds for their children such as savings bonds and education IRAs. Also, financial aid, grants and loans are plentiful and available to anyone who has a desire and meets the criteria for aid. Georgia offers a unique educational program to its high school students called the HOPE (Helping Outstanding Students Educationally) Scholarship. High school students qualify to receive the HOPE Scholarship funds if they earn a "B" average throughout high school and maintain a "B" average during college. Academic and sport scholarships are also available to high school students. The academic scholarships are based on students' grade point averages, and sport scholarships are based on students' sport performance and grade point averages. These scholarships are usually funded throughout students' college careers.

While the number of traditional college students increases every year, the most dramatic rise in student population is in the non-traditional student category. There are many non-traditional students attending college today, especially forty-year-olds. Many older students decide to attend or return to college for personal growth, better jobs and sometimes for knowledge. Attending college after high school offers many advantages; however, it requires extra effort for older students. Some older students are married with children. Extra time is spent assisting their children with homework, attending PTA meetings, doctor appointments, sports, and other activities. Many older students have full- or part-time jobs. Their work schedules require them to work from twenty to forty hours a week. Therefore, they have limited time for studying. Some older students study before commuting to work, on the job, riding MARTA, and during breaks. In addition, they have financial burdens: paying rent, utilities, health and auto insurance, telephone, groceries, and work-related expenses such as gas and lunch. In the meantime, they have to add tuition and books to their list of expenses.

Since many older students have not attended college, they have to make attitude adjustments. Older students have to make sacrifices and give up some of life's pleasures, such as watching television, entertaining, and reading mystery and romance novels. These students are sometimes required to take remedial courses because of inadequate scores on placement tests. They spend their time perusing books on how to study, how to take college exams, and how to move from a career into college. Older students have to prepare themselves for exams by taking good notes and asking questions during class time. Most older college students do not know how to get started to prepare for college, what to expect or whether they have the ability to graduate. In addition, older students should ask for assistance, support and guidance from their professors, counselor, tutorial labs, and classmates. Furthermore, colleges offer free tutoring, personal computers and free Internet to students.

While older students have to put forth extra effort to attend college, good planning is equally important to older students' success. Students have to make adjustments to their work and family schedules. Many students attend school during week nights although they can also attend school on weekends or at sites that are more convenient to their homes. Most campus libraries are open seven days a week. Many colleges offer telecourses or online courses to students. These courses are completed in the privacy of their own homes through the Internet. These course alternatives are great for older students on a schedule or students who do not want to travel to campuses across town.

In addition, older college students should seek support from their employers and families. More and more companies are setting up computers in their employees' homes. Employees can work any time as long as they meet established deadlines. Also, they can ask employers to allow them to attend school during working hours or lunch breaks. Many employers will allow their employees flexibility to attend college. Some employees come to work early, take work home to earn extra hours during the week, or use annual leave to attend classes. Even more important, older students depend on their family members for help with their children or pets. Students often need their spouse, parents, or siblings to temporarily assume their responsibilities to pick up their children from school or daycare and to nurture the pets.

The traditional college students that are eighteen will probably always outnumber non-traditional students who are forty returning to or attending college for the first time. However, college is a good idea regardless of one's age. Older students today have proven that college is for them, too, if they are willing to put forth the extra effort and good planning to succeed.

FINAL OUTLINE
College: Eighteen or Forty

Thesis: While attending college can be rewarding for eighteen-year-olds, at the age of forty, it requires extra effort and good planning.

I.   It can be rewarding for traditional students to attend college when they are eighteen.
   A. Attending college after high school has personal advantages.
      1. Eighteen-year-olds live at home and have fewer financial responsibilities.
      2. Eighteen-year-olds can attend classes any time.
   B. Attending college after high school can be monetarily rewarding.
      1. High school students work a part-time job.
      2. High school students' parents plan and set aside funds for their education.
      3. Financial aid, grants and loans are available to high school students.
      4. Maintaining a "B" average throughout high school guarantees the HOPE Scholarship.
      5. Academic and sport scholarships are available to high school students.
II.   Attending college at age forty requires extra effort.
   A. Many people with other responsibilities decide to attend college in their forties.
      1. Older college students are often married and have children.
      2. Older college students have full-time jobs.
         a. They have less time to study.
         b. They have financial burdens.
   B. Many older students have to make attitude adjustments.
      1. Older college students have to learn how to study effectively.
      2. Older college students have to learn to prepare for exams.

        3. Older college students have to learn to ask for assistance.

III.   Attending college at age forty requires good planning.
    A. Older college students should make adjustments to their work and family schedules.
       1. Older college students can attend school on weekends or on other campus sites.
       2. Older college students can take telecourses or online courses.
    B. Older college students should ask for support from their employers and families.
       1. They should ask employers to set up computers in their homes to meet established deadlines.
       2. They should ask employers to allow them to attend school during working hours or lunch breaks.
       3. They should ask family members for help with their children or pets.

Analysis of the Magazine *Maxim*

By Herman Miller

English 1101: Analysis

As he tries to escape the evil compound without tearing his tuxedo, our hero finds himself trapped between a pit of sharks and a squad of henchmen. He notices that they have his girlfriend, who just happens to be a supermodel. He raises his hands as if in defeat and uses his cufflinks to take out the squad of goons. He rescues the girl just as the base's self-destruct is armed. Kicking down doors and jumping across sinkholes, they come across a submarine. Seconds after they are on their way in the state-of-the-art submarine, the compound bursts into flames. As our hero reports to headquarters with the status of the mission and a dry but witty joke, his now half-dressed supermodel girlfriend opens a bottle of champagne. Everything fades to black. Reality returns to our hero as he grabs an issue of *Maxim* off the shelf and walks to the checkout. Our hero is better known as "Mister Joe Average."

Joe Average is exactly who he sounds to be. He does not have an amazing job or a super fast car, and he definitely does not have a supermodel girlfriend. He is male, 18-35, with an average education. While many different types of people read *Maxim,* the target audience is narrowed down to Joe Average. The magazine works very hard to appeal to the consumer group of the everyday man.

Sexual innuendo, interesting sport phrases, and facts about the latest gadgets decorate the sides of the cover to intrigue the consumer. These teasers drop promises of hidden secrets about women and how to be more like James Bond, and they add a large dose of celebrity name-dropping. The teasers are written with liberty to draw in as many readers as possible. If the story is about

74

making your car run better, the teaser might say, "What revs her engine." *Maxim* cleverly uses sex to lure the male consumer.

Just like the teasers, pictures of today's most popular sex symbols shroud the cover. The models may be dressed in a tight dress or a nightgown, but most models hardly wear anything. Models wearing bikinis, lingerie, or nearly nothing are on the cover to catch the reader's attention. These women give the camera a lusty stare so the consumer feels he is the object of the model's affection. Sometimes the models on the cover are more than enough reason to buy the magazine. Music groups, athletes, and fast cars on the cover are not enough for most men.

The entire magazine, from cover to cover, is male oriented. Even the ads are made to appeal to more men. Pictures of women drinking, trucks driving in the mud, and men talking while having some beers are on every other page. The women in the ads normally wear sexy little outfits in bars or on the street, yet sometimes the ladies may only be wearing bikinis on the beach. It seems the pictures rarely have anything to do with the product. One ad has a woman walking on the beach in her swimsuit and holding a cell phone. Apparently, the ad was for a long distance carrier. Another ad had women surrounding a man just to see his watch. Even with the understanding that ads have little basis in reality, a lot of men are interested in the idea that a watch or a long distance carrier will make them more attractive.

Between the ads, the articles lie in wait. They discuss everything from how-to tips to the cover story. Popular articles include the "he says/ she says" pages, the sex tips, and the cover story. "He says/ she says" gives the man's point of view as well as the woman's. Most of the topics they discuss are about sex. The sex tips just give advice from doctors, therapists, and even sex "professionals." Advice is given on everything from how to dress when going on a date to tricks of the trade in the bedroom. The cover story is always about the model on the cover. *Maxim* often likes to discuss what type of men interest her, her sexual preferences, and even her sex stories. All are very informative and interesting to read for everyone, yet they are aimed towards men.

The articles do not all focus on sex. There are some about sports, movies, and fashion. All the articles are well written. They use day-to-day language so everyone can easily understand.

Maxim clearly understands its target audience. The editors understand that men enjoy sports, cars, and funny jokes, but they also understand that men hold sex on a shelf above that. Maxim draws in a lot of readers because they understand men will always be interested in sex. It may sound shallow and perverted to say sex sells Maxim, but it is the honest truth. While Home And Garden sells recipes and vacuuming tips and YM sells teen idols and dream guys, Maxim sells the pure old-fashioned need for sex. They are selling the "who, what, where, when, and how" when it comes to sex, and men are buying it by the pound. It does not matter what they do, how much money they have, or who they are. Mister Joe Average will always be interested in sex. While the idea of finding out how to meet Mark McGuire is interesting to some men, the simple ideas of sex and sex-related topics are enough to draw in most consumers. However, Maxim does talk about sports, cars, and many other topics that men enjoy. It sticks to the idea printed on the stem of the cover: "The best thing to happen to men since women."

Smoke Signals: An Act of Forgiveness

By Shirley Bennett

ENGL 1101: Film Analysis

Smoke Signals is a heart-felt drama in which director Chris Eyre takes an almost forgotten society, the Native American Indian, and demonstrates through character development and narration those universal emotions that are caused by the rippling effect of misunderstanding, guilt, and forgiveness.

The film opens in Idaho, on the Coeur d' Alene Indian reservation, where we are introduced to the ancient Indian tradition of story telling. Through a powerful style of narration by Thomas Builds-the-Fire (Evan Adams), we learn of a fire that "rose up like General George Armstrong Custer" and swallowed up Thomas' parents. Arnold Joseph (Gary Farmer), the father of Victor Joseph (Adam Beach), saved Thomas from the fate of the fire. Thus, we learn of a common thread of pain that binds the lives of Thomas and Victor: "There are some children who aren't really children at all; they are just pillars of flame that burn everything they touch. And there are some children who are just pillars of ash that fall apart if you touch them." Thomas and Victor were children born of flame and ash.

Victor's father is tormented by the fire's secret, and for years he tries to vanish into a bottle of beer. Finally, unable to bear his suppressed pain, Arnold leaves the reservation and, ultimately, twelve-year-old Victor. Like most children growing up without their fathers, Victor has learned to blame himself for his father's leaving. He is angry at the world, and his anger has been misdirected towards Thomas. And Thomas, a goofy, imaginative, want-to-be medicine man, has accepted his role as Victor's forever faithful and forgiving verbal punching bag.

77

After learning of his father's death, Victor intends to go to Arizona in order to collect his father's belongings; however, short of money, Thomas convinces Victor that he will pay for the trip, but only if he can go along. One has to wonder why Thomas wanted to go. Was he there to help Victor face the truth? Perhaps Thomas was in some way Victor's spiritual guide. The message isn't clear; however, one thing is certain. It was Thomas who made the journey enjoyable for the viewers.

The journey to Arizona is a typical road trip with the familiar pattern of polar opposite personalities who are forced to put up with each other yet in the end learn to respect each other. However, in addition, this road trip takes viewers on a humorous and hard-hitting emotional journey that jumps from present-day events to childhood flashbacks and includes dialogue that is infused with truths, wisdom, and Native American dry humor that pokes fun at references to historical and celebrity figures. For example, "It's a good day to die; it's a good day to have breakfast."

Throughout the journey, Eyre effectively takes viewers on an emotional roller coaster ride. One moment you are smiling as Thomas repeatedly spins fictitious tales of humor, and in the next moment you are feeling the unexpressed yet obvious pain of Victor and his father. As the movie progresses, so does Victor's pain and understanding. The pivotal point in the movie is when Victor is forced to confront his father's death. Susie Song (Irene Bedard) is the neighbor that found Victor's father. She is the keeper of secrets and, ultimately, the pathway to a truth that Victor must face about his father. Thus, the mood of the movie shifts from soft comedy to hard-hitting drama. However, it is not until Victor and Thomas are headed back to the reservation that Victor is finally able to begin the purging process of releasing anger and relinquishing childhood illusions. It begins when a drunk driver, who is the personification of Victor's father, causes a vehicle accident.

Victor aggressively and emotionally expresses his anger towards the drunk driver by repeatedly stating, "Look what you have done." Obviously, this is what he longed to tell his father. In

78

the next scene, Victor runs for medical assistance. Against the darkness of night, he experiences a progressive series of mental flashbacks pertaining to his father's life, the house fire, and Susie Song's message of truth. After finally dropping from exhaustion, Victor has an illusive vision of his father that begins the emotional healing process. In the final scenes, a haunting impression of Victor's final act of mourning lingers as the narration takes viewers on a reflective journey.

Smoke Signals is a low-budget movie with great acting and a haunting sound track of Indian chants. Unfortunately, it has a sluggish beginning. The reason for this is due to the unnecessary interjections of ineffective humor intended to illustrate the Indian way of life. However, once Victor and Thomas take to the road, the pace begins to pick up. The character development of Thomas Builds-the-Fire has a slow methodical rhythm that embraces the viewer, as does the movie's narrative style, which could be compared to *The Shawshank Redemption*. The narration, which is delivered by Evan Adams, has a sharp edge of wisdom and makes a profound point. For example, "I think we are all traveling heavy with illusions" delivers a universal truth and encapsulates the theme of *Smoke Signals*. Ultimately, this is a movie about forgiveness. We are asked, "How do we forgive our fathers?" Maybe by watching *Smoke Signals* we can begin our own process of personal forgiveness. This is a must-see movie for anyone who has ever had a conflict with his or her father.

The Burning in His Heart

By Sally Chase Palmer

English 1101: Film Analysis

Smoke Signals, an independent film directed by Chris Eyre, takes a glimpse into the harsh reality of a Native American reservation.   From the main characters to the descriptive background, Eyre's insight into the hearts and minds of this culture is magnificent. With its comedy and tragedy carefully interwoven throughout the movie, *Smoke Signals* eloquently follows the journey of a young man as well as the journey of a culture.

The opening scene grabs your attention with a grim scene of a home on a reservation engulfed in flames on the night of July 4, 1976, the 200th anniversary of America's independence from England.   This is the first example of Eyre's superb ability to symbolically embrace the contrast between Native American heritage and culture and modern-day America.   As the camera focuses on the burning home, suddenly a baby is thrown out of the window. A brave neighbor, Arnold Joseph (Gary Farmer), lunges forward and captures the baby in his arms. Arnold is later described as the father of the main character, Victor Joseph (Adam Beach), who ventures out on a quest for truth.

As the film changes from 1976 to 1998, Victor, now a young adult, accompanied by a childhood friend, Thomas Builds-the-Fire (Evan Adams), sets out on a journey and discovers that the original intention of his trip, to claim the body of his deceased father, turns into a journey of self-discovery. Victor, the main character, is angry and confused about his father's death because his only memories of Arnold Joseph are those of an abusive, alcoholic father. Thomas, on the other hand, has fond memories of Arnold.   This sets up a struggle between Victor and Thomas that

80

continues throughout the movie. In depicting this struggle, the director also encompasses the struggle between the "white man's world" and Native American culture. Comical references of irony, combined with the dark history of the clash of these two cultures, are described in the characters' daily lives. In one scene, as Victor and Thomas are walking down the road that leads out of the reservation, two Native American women stop and give them a ride. At the edge of the reservation, the car stops, and the women let the two travelers out of the car. Tauntingly, they shout out the window, "Hey boys, don't forget your passports!" Thomas is confused and asks, "Why?" They retort, "You're going off the Rez [reservation], aren't you?" With this innocent but mindful comment, Eyre lightheartedly explains the caution American Indians take against the prejudice and distrust that often greet them when merging with modern American culture.

Another more subtle example of prejudice is shown when the two boys are traveling on a bus. As Thomas and Victor board a bus, you see the white bus driver's hand gripping a handle to close the door. The scene moves from the bus driver's hand to the expression on his face as he looks disapprovingly at them. Once again, Eyre uses his symbolism to unmask the cancer of racism in our society.

Throughout their trip, the film continually flashes back to the boys' younger years. In depicting the life of one Native American, Victor Joseph, the film points out the horrific living conditions on a reservation, the prevalence of alcoholism among their culture, and the loss of spiritual heritage. Finally arriving at their destination, Victor discovers truths about his father he denounces at first, but he soon discovers that facing the truth releases him from the self-bondage that he has kept himself in all of his life. The director's reference to "facing the truth" is exemplified in Thomas' comment, "We are all traveling heavy with illusions." This film encapsulates the word "journey" in every sense. With its wit, seriousness, irony and symbolism, this film brilliantly describes triumph over tragedy.

Open Adoption Is the Best Way

By Mendi Sandoz

English 1101: Argument, Researched

The adoption debate affects nearly 25 million Americans who have either been adopted, adopted a child, or have given a child up for adoption (Knickerbocker 1). In the early days of American society, open adoption was the standard procedure for adoption, yet as time has passed, almost every state has adopted laws requiring closed books. Presently, at the dawn of a new millennium, the adoption debate is red hot with advocates stressing the individual rights of all parties involved. The Constitutional rights of all Americans should be upheld, yet I believe that the rights of the adopted child should be first priority. Although many people are against open adoption, I favor the policy because it encourages people to give up children for adoption, is better for the birthparents, and, most importantly, increases the successful adjustment of children who have been adopted.

Some say that open adoption does not provide the opportunity for adoptive parents to pass their own values to their adopted children. However, adoptive parents still have complete custody and control over their adopted children under the open method until the age of eighteen. Others maintain that open adoption causes adoptees to become confused by the knowledge of two sets of parents. On the contrary, people adopted under the open system tend to have a better emotional state than those adopted in a closed system. Still others argue that closed adoption systems give the adoptive parents more opportunity to establish a stable, protective environment. But, under an open adoption system, the adoptive parents are given even more control over the future of their child by outlining the contact between the birthparent and the child.

Under a friendlier, open system for adoption, women carrying children they cannot raise will be more open to the idea of adoption. In Kansas, the only state that never has closed adoption records, the rate of adoption is higher than other surrounding states (Knickerbocker 1). When birthparents feel that they can have at least some control over their child, whether through contact by letters, meeting the birthparents, or by making their medical records available to the child, they are more likely to feel confident that their child will be well cared for. According to Candis McLean, adoption experts believe that as open adoption becomes more widely known, more parents will come to recognize adoption as an alternative to abortion and young or single parenthood (32).

Many birthmothers after giving up their children for adoption feel a large sense of hurt and depression. According to Annette Baron and Reuben Pannor, clinical social workers, under a closed system of adoption, birthparents "do not know who adopted their child, where he or she lives or even if the child is dead or alive" (230). Without any kind of knowledge of their child, the birthparents may fear that the adopted children may hate and despise them (230). This fear does not allow healing for the birthparents. Open adoption allows birthparents to be comforted by the fact that their children are living in a loving home. Periodic updates give the birthparents relief knowing that their child is well cared for (Siegel 15).

Children who are given up for adoption face many tough circumstances that other children do not face. The feelings of loss and abandonment that adoptees face are only increased by the secrecy and anonymity of closed adoptions (Baran and Pannor 234). In an open adoption system, adoptees' feelings of rejection can be greatly diminished. The continuing link with the birthparents dispels the thoughts that they were abandoned and forgotten (Baran and Pannor 235). According to Scott Baldauf, adoptive parents Steve Daggett and Diana Gilpatrick believe that maintaining an open relationship with their son's birthparents will help him avoid some of the emotional problems that affect most adopted children (3). One of the biggest fears of adopted people is that their birthparents do not love or care for them and have abandoned them to the cold, cruel world. With an open system of adoption, adoptees can avoid this feeling by learning the circumstances resulting in their being given up for adoption and making the adoption process beneficial for all parties involved.

Open adoption is the most preferable form of adoption because it is better for the birthparents and adopted children, and it also encourages people to give up children for adoption rather than have abortions, knowing that they can have a long-term relationship with their child. Open adoption is better for all parties involved because it avoids the secrecy and the resultant fear that secrecy brings. Many states have now realized the positive nature of open adoption policies and have taken legislative action to make records accessible to all who need to see them.

Works Cited

Baldauf, Scott. "Adoption With an Open Door for Birth Parents." Christian Science Monitor 21 October 1998: B3.

Baran, Annette and Reuben Pannor. "An Open Adoption Policy Is Best." Adoption: Opposing Viewpoints. Eds. David Bender and Bruno Leone. San Diego: Greenhaven Press, 1995. 102-106.

McLean, Candis. "How to Rehabilitate Adoption." Alberta Report 24 August 1998: 32.

Knickerbocker, Brad. "Birth Mothers Battle to Keep Records Closed." Christian Science Monitor 16 December 1998: 1.

Siegel, Deborah H. "Open Adoption of Infants: Adoptive Parents' Perceptions of Advantages and Disadvantages." Social Work January 1993: 15.

Ordinarily, I do my grocery shopping at Sevananda, a natural foods cooperative in Little Five Points. A couple of months ago, however, I noticed a slight change in many of the products they carry. As I strolled down the cereal aisle, I saw a sunny yellow box of corn flakes with a bright blue "NON-GMO" label stamped on the front of the box in the same style as if it were advertising that it was "New and Improved" or contained "30% more, FREE." On the next aisle, I turned over a bag of potato chips to check out its ingredients and found a statement in bold print preceding the list claiming that all ingredients were not genetically modified. During this shopping trip, I noticed several more such labels on products ranging from soymilk to candy bars. The following week, I took a brief trip to Kroger. While browsing its aisles, I noticed virtually no products labeled as GMO-free. The absence of these labels struck me as odd and prompted me to research the subject of GMOs. Judging by the facts I found, I have come to the conclusion that GMOs are potentially unsafe for human consumption. They should be thoroughly tested for safety, and all products containing them should be clearly labeled.

So what is a GMO and why do some companies seem to be so proud not to carry them while others ignore the issue? As Warren Thayer writes in *Frozen Food Age*, "[. . .] GMO foods (also known as genetically engineered or GE foods) have been genetically modified to grow bigger, faster, stronger and/or with less pesticide" (34). For example, the gene of a tomato has been spliced with that of a salmon in order for the tomato to take on the salmon's ability to endure cold weather. Genetic modification of crops makes the farmer's work much easier because he will have

85

more freedom in his farming methods and a more perfect crop by industry standards. Bt-modified crops have been very popular with farmers in recent years. Bt is a bacteria used as a pesticide by organic farmers. It is killed by sunlight, so it leaves no residue. However, when engineered into the DNA of a crop such as corn, it remains as part of the plant; therefore, the EPA registers Bt crops as pesticides instead of plants. The majority of such crops are not fed to humans directly but are instead used as livestock feed. Warren Thayer writes, "[T]oday's grain storage and handling industry is not set up to segregate GMO from non-GMO. Everything is commingled, and there are no real audit trails back to the farm" (36). This demonstrates a possibility of Bt corn and other GM crops not suitable for human consumption appearing in just about any conventional product on the market.

Genetically engineered organisms pose a serious threat to the environment. Pollen and soil cannot be contained within one certain area. The two remain as possible avenues for outside crop contamination. Warren Thayer once again makes a good point: "GMO's may also pose a serious threat to organic products. For example, GMO crops can crossbreed with native weeds and/or non-GMO crops. Corn pollen travels far. It will be difficult to keep non-GMO crops pure" (36).

Another concern is the "round-up ready" and other herbicide-resistant crops. "Round-up ready" crops have been engineered to be resistant to the herbicide round-up in order for the farmers to be able to spray this chemical liberally on their crops. This modification presents a few problems. First, weeds eventually form a resistance to the herbicide, causing the development of "super weeds" (similar to the "super viruses" that antibiotics have created). The second problem is the excess of chemicals that the farmers will be free to use considering that it will have no effects on the crops themselves. An increase in herbicide application on the crops we consume equals a larger amount of chemicals we ingest. The final problem is in the soil. Rain and irrigation water spread these herbicides into other, possibly organic, fields, making them unusable to those farmers.

The chemicals are also spread into rivers and lakes, contaminating our food and water supply.

Humans are not the only creatures affected by this careless farming method. The insect community, such as butterflies and honey bees, have been seriously injured or killed by such practices. It was discovered in 1999 that monarch butterflies died from feeding off a milkweed plant dusted with the pollen of Bt corn (Mothers 9). This is an alarming discovery that demonstrates the health risks of GMOs for humans as well as the environment. For one thing, if a substance kills off one creature, there is a chance that it holds some toxicity to humans. Also, when there is a threat to the life of any part of the earth's delicate ecosystem, there is a threat to us. Although insects are almost at the opposite end of the food chain from us, it is only a matter of time before we feel the effects.

Another frightening aspect of genetic engineering is the fact that it has gone virtually untested for health safety, yet Americans buy products with genetically engineered ingredients every day. In fact, according to Elizabeth Parle, "[T]he global market for transgenic crop products grew rapidly from 1995 to 1999. Global sales estimated at $75 million in 1995 reached 1.6 billion in 1998, and increased to an estimated $2.1 billion in 1999 [. . .] (10). These products may be cheaper and easier to produce, but they are being bought blindly. The majority of the American public is clueless as to what a GMO really is, yet they buy these products and consume them daily. Although negotiations are still ongoing, in 1999 food manufacturers and retailers in Europe pledged not to carry GMO-containing products (Rogers 26). These countries did not come to this decision without good reason. The suspicion of possible health risks is well founded.

The wariness that European nations show towards GMOs stems from the hesitation of the companies that produced them to test their safety. There is a multitude of ways that the DNA splicing procedure could create problems. It is unknown whether a certain combination of genetic material could lessen a plant's nutritional value, create an allergen, or become carcinogenic.

87

These qualities can either be recognized by laboratory testing now or once it's too late and the effects have already injured or taken lives. A good example of this phenomenon is the incident involving tryptophan, a naturally occurring sleep-inducing amino acid. Unfortunately, during the process by which the bacteria produced the tryptophan, a toxin was also produced which resulted in 37 deaths and 1500 cases of partial paralysis (Karp 7). Even considering this mistake, manufacturers avoid conducting tests, which should make the public wonder what these companies have to hide. The refusal couldn't be due to a lack of funding, because the genetic engineering itself is very costly, so apparently money is not an issue. Even if it is, shouldn't health come before profit? It should, but in this day and age, public safety seems to be ignored until a problem manifests itself, risking bad press for that company. Then and only then is the problem addressed, because that company risks losing money.

The public should feel free to question the secrecy that companies such as Monsanto--which was the company that introduced the first GMO, round-up ready soybeans in 1996 and remains the leader in genetic modification--hold regarding their creations. It is our duty as consumers to demand fair treatment and know the product we're paying for. It should be absolutely mandatory for manufacturers to thoroughly test new products, especially those which have an experimental, artificial element to them. The labeling of genetically modified products should not even need to be requested. If new ingredients are added to the food we eat, we have a right to know. Presently, the only way to truly be sure that what we eat is pure is to eat only organic produce and products which advertise no GMO ingredients.

It is my belief that the type of technology used to genetically alter organisms, whether it is crops or animals, is disastrous in human hands. By nature, we are too greedy and selfish to have control of such a powerful thing as nature. There is no wondering about this technology falling into the wrong hands; it has been there all along. Humans have no right to fool with nature by altering the ecosystem to suit our fancies. The earth is not something to control; it is only to be observed and appreciated.

Works Cited

Karp, Harvey. "Ask the Doctor." <u>Safe Food News</u> Sept. 2000: 7.

Mothers for Natural Law. "From Soil to Superviruses." <u>Safe Food News</u> Sept. 2000: 9.

Parle, Elizabeth. "GM crops: More Food, or Thought?" <u>Chemical Market Reporter</u> 20 March 2000: 10-12.

Rogers, Paul. "The GMO Show." <u>Candy Industry</u> Aug. 1999: 26-34.

Thayer, Warren. "Pardon, Is That a Fish Gene in Your Veggies?" <u>Frozen Food Age</u> March 2000: 34-6.

Topic: Archaeologists have learned much about the lives of first-century Romans from the excavations of houses buried by lava at Pompeii. Suppose that your home were preserved just as it is now. What conclusions about modern life might this evidence lead future archaeologists to draw?

Were an archaeologist in a future time to discover the preserved ruins of my house, (s)he could clearly infer three things. First, (s)he would observe that contemporary society is largely family oriented. Next, the archaeologist would see that, to an extent, curiosity and interest regarding foreign cultures abound. Last, a future archaeologist would discover that, while not so to the extent of our own ancestors, we tend towards physical activity, especially in our leisure time. With these discoveries, (s)he would have a clearer picture and understanding of contemporary American life.

In the basement of my home, which is the most often intact portion of ruined structures, one would find toys and games. While some children's toys are newly developed, others are quite basic, the concepts of which have been little changed since antiquity. That said, future peoples would clearly understand that these toys, to them relics, were meant for children. They would find many such toys and games, along with pictures of generations of my family. These discoveries would clearly indicate a sense of family importance and solidarity to the investigative researcher.

In addition to family items, the future archaeologist would discover an extended library of texts, with subjects ranging from economies of other nations to the dress and personal habits of foreign cultures. (S)he would find memorabilia from my family's journeys abroad, and (s)he would also discover a wide ranging collection of foreign religious texts. The archaeologist would infer from these finds that there was in existence a deep and abiding interest in the varying and colorful cultures of our diverse world.

Third, the archaeologist would observe all manner of sporting equipment. From what (s)he might otherwise infer, (s)he may come to the correct conclusion that an active leisure lifestyle was common among our contemporary population. The archaeologist would discover equipment for sports such as baseball, football, racquetball and basketball, as well as equipment for hunting and fishing. While the researcher might understandably mistake some items for weapons of either war or defense, most of the items in evidence would most probably be clearly identified as sporting tools and equipment, as surely some forms of contemporary sporting events and activities would survive into the future.

A future archaeologist would see, in an excavation of the future ruins of my home, that my family is actively pursuant of physical recreation in our leisure time, is avidly interested in learning about cultures in our world community, and is oriented towards family care, security and development. With these discoveries, the future archaeological researcher might gain some understanding of the modern life of not only my family, but of mainstream Western culture as a whole.

Actual Regents' Test Essay

By Adam Bost

Rating: 4

Topic: **If you were going to a foreign country, would you rather go with a tour group or on your own? Explain.**

During my years on this planet, I have been fortunate to be able to travel to several foreign countries. I have found that the best way to see a foreign country, especially if it is your first time, is with a tour group. Being a part of a tour group gives you freedoms from the many tasks involved in the planning and administration of a trip to a foreign country. A tour group provides many advantages when traveling such as crossing the language barriers, providing for a safe and comfortable visit, and finding the best hotels, restaurants, and activities to make your trip a success.

As a part of a tour group, you are no longer left to fend for yourself in a place that doesn't speak your language. In fact, most travel agencies have guides that not only live in the country you are visiting, but also speak the language of both that country and your own. This allows for a great advantage on your part because you now have an in with not only the language, but also the native customs. Only in a tour group do you find yourself no longer in the dark when it comes to simply talking to the natives.

A second advantage in being a part of a tour group is closely related to the first. A tour group provides for a safe and comfortable visit to foreign countries. Tour companies have planned hundreds of tours and are knowledgeable as to unsafe areas that may harvest [sic] high crime or other illegal activities. They can plan a trip that is not only exciting but will get you home in one piece.

Finally, tour groups take the responsibility of finding hotels, restaurants, and suitable activities for you during your stay. Not only are you relieved of this stress, you are also insured that the tour company knows the area well and can find the best, safest, and, most importantly, the most affordable accommodations. On top of everything, all you have to worry about is having a good time.

Traveling to foreign countries can be thrilling and adventurous or dangerous and stressful. If one chooses to go at it alone, then Godspeed, but I would recommend a tour group. A tour group provides many advantages such as guides and translators, providing a safe visit, and finding the best accommodations without having the hassle of finding them yourself. My suggestion is to use a tour group for at least your first few trips out of the country. You will find it to be a much more relaxing experience. Happy traveling!

Topic: If you could take one entire year off from your responsibilities of school or work, how would you spend that year? Explain why you would make these choices.

When viewing horror films or sci-fi pictures, movie critics tell us to suspend disbelief. If given the opportunity to spend an entire year away from my work and school responsibilities, I would first have to suspend disbelief--a disbelief that there actually *is* a world outside the rigors of school and the banalities of work. Amazement and trepidation aside, I would set out on the cliched and often parodied task of "finding myself."

My year would begin with a trip to the post office for a passport. Shirking school for a year would mean I'd have to educate myself. And what better way to do that than by participating in a little globetrotting? First stop: Europe, where I'd finally see all of the landmarks my history professors keep talking about and visit the graves of the wise old sages my English professors croon about. I think next I'd journey to Australia to kickbox with kangaroos and swim along the coral reefs. I'm sure I could become enlightened by all of the mystique of the Orient and become enthralled with my own personal Latin music explosion in South America. All the while, I would rekindle my passion for photography and collect a mass of pictorial eye candy for rainy days when my year of self discovery has ended.

During my travels, I would read every book on my long list of "books to read when I have time off." I would watch every movie I never get a chance to watch, and I would rededicate myself to learning some really fun tricks on inline skates. But the most important pastime that would occupy the days of my year of freedom would be a concerted effort to figure out this whole Internet thing.

When I'm not traveling the world or overhauling my senses with immersion in media, I imagine I'll be spending a lot of time with old friends and family. It will be through them that I do the majority of my self discovery. This is because it is only through our connections to the past that we have any sense of what our future is to become, to paraphrase one of the sages whose grave I'll surely visit.

All of this self discovery and globetrotting will no doubt wear on me, and I will probably take up a soothing and handy trade like crochet or underwater basket weaving. At the end of my year, I will have acquired enough souvenirs, photos, and worldly knowledge to last a lifetime. But it will be the memories of the experiences that lead me to write the memoirs of my youth. The book will be published and make it onto "Oprah," and Hollywood will beckon to develop these fantastic stories into a movie. So vast the knowledge gained and the experiences shared will be, that movie critics everywhere will review it and warn the average moviegoer that this film--this amazing bundle of life's joys--must be approached with a suspension of disbelief.

Electoral College: The Un-American Way

By Daniel Proto
English 1102: Argument, Researched

National pride is an aspect of American life that is very difficult to overlook. We as a people are proud of many things: our economy, our culture, our national defense forces, and--though at times we may not particularly like those people residing there-- our system of government. Democracy is simply a way of life to the average American citizen, and any other way of choosing a ruler seems just plain wrong. However, there is one aspect of our government that does not reflect the country's sentiments of being run as a true democracy. Strangely enough, this aspect just happens to involve the most powerful office in the land. The system currently employed to elect our single highest official, the President of the United States, does not rest on a true principle of the people ruling. Rather, there exists a sort of buffer zone, created by our founding fathers for a variety of reasons, between the will of the people and the office of the President. This barrier has come to be known as the Electoral College, and in recent times it has been attacked on nearly every front possible. The Electoral College in its current incarnation does nothing but prevent the true will of the people from being felt, and there are a host of alternatives that could be incorporated to better focus the true light of democracy in America.

The Electoral College was originally established to address certain concerns held by this country's forefathers. These reservations must first be examined before the true problems with our current system of Presidential election can be fully understood. As stated by Yale Law School Southmayd Chair holder Akhil Amar in his testimony before a House committee on election reform, "[T]he so-called electoral college [was] a brilliant

99

eighteenth century device that cleverly solved a cluster of eighteenth century problems." There were essentially three of these problems that the College sought to circumvent. First, the framers of the Constitution felt that the average citizen would not possess enough vital information concerning the country and the world as a whole in order to make delicate decisions such as who should be sent into the Oval Office (Cummings 54). Means of communication in the eighteenth century were not nearly as efficient as those found in our society today, and so oftentimes news would lag weeks or even months behind.

This situation of delay and lack of knowledge also tied into the constitutional framers' second area of concern: that the people of our nation could be swayed by the persuasive words of a local demagogue (Amar). This possibility was a great fear held by our founding fathers, as they were highly opposed to any form of "mob rule" or an election system that "invit[ed] demagoguery and possibly dictatorship as one man claimed to represent the Voice of the American People" (Amar). However, a slate of well-educated electors would be immune to this phenomenon of grass roots, tear-jerking candidates.

Finally, our forefathers lived in a time of heavy states' rights sentiment. A direct popular election would favor the large states or possibly those states that desired to gain more clout by allowing women or even slaves to vote. Wanting to keep each state as even with its peers as possible, the drafters of the Constitution created the Electoral College to avoid "upset[ting] a careful balance of power among the states" (Amar). As can be seen, the College validly addressed the concerns of those creating our system of presidential election. However, in recent times it has become obvious that a reform is necessary.

The reasons for reform are many and readily apparent and show that the eighteenth century concerns addressed by the College are no longer a serious threat to representative democracy in America. The most obvious advance made since the writing of the Constitution deals with voting rights. No longer is the right to vote reserved only for wealthy, white, land-owning citizens.

Through the fifteenth and nineteenth amendments, blacks and women respectively have been granted their constitutional right to be represented fairly in government (Cummings A-11, 12). Thus, the possible unbalancing of the states through shady population-related voting tactics is no longer a valid argument for keeping the College in place.

Moving on to the next concern held by our forefathers that is no longer an issue, the days of slow-moving information and news are gone. With the introduction of radio, television, and the Internet, information on nearly any topic can be had in a matter of minutes, not weeks. Our populace is as well-informed on current events and presidential information nowadays as is any state-selected elector. We as a people are ready to accept the responsibility of choosing our own leader in a more direct fashion than the Electoral College.

Regarding our founding fathers' third concern, a well connected and informed populace makes the chance of a regional demagogue rising to power a slim one. Even if a presidential candidate is able to effectively use grass roots campaigning to play on the wants of locals in one area of the country, the rest of the nation will see him for what he truly is, and his quest for the presidency will be cut short. In essence, America has moved beyond its stages of infancy into a booming adulthood, and as is customary for those coming of age in our society today, our country should now assume its long-awaited freedoms and responsibilities.

Also, the College has itself created a new and very dangerous problem in presidential elections that must be addressed very soon. The Electoral College has become so grossly unfair and inefficient that it has begun generating its own list of problems, foremost among these being the "winner-take-all" mentality of the American electoral system (Sung). This problem can be showcased by the fact that even if a Presidential candidate were to "carry"—i.e. win—the popular election in a state by only one vote, he would still receive every single one of that state's electoral ballots. Thus, the will of the very slim majority is felt, while the voices of the minority are completely ignored. This phenomenon creates a system of drastic majority rule. However, many political scientists and respected political thinkers—even those in favor of keeping the Electoral College in its current form—are quick to point out that "majority rule is not the principle of our Constitution. Rather it is majority rule with minority consent" (Best). The will of *all* the people must be felt in America for our democracy to function properly. The College distorts this will by giving weight only to the opinions of those in the majority. The minority is no longer able to check the clout of the majority, and thus there is little preventing this majority from allotting itself increasing degrees of power. After all, as long as those in the majority are able to keep themselves at least one vote ahead of their counterparts, then they have little in the way of being overthrown to worry about. Luckily, there are so very many issues in America that all citizens see themselves as a member of the minority in at least one instance, and thus the power of the majority has so far been limited. However, even this point showcases the need for electoral reform. After all, if every American is in some way a minority, then should the will of the minority not be given more weight?

This question has been asked by many people, as the idea of replacing the Electoral College is shared by many prominent government officials, university professors, and—most importantly—common citizens. However, there are two major schools of thought as to which new system of presidential election would best reflect the democratic will of the people. First among these replacement methods is the idea of instituting a direct popular election. More specifically, the system of Instant Runoff Voting (IRV) is a highly supported proposition. In essence, IRV would call for the President to be elected based strictly on the popular vote. However, IRV would also require that a Presidential candidate receive a majority of this popular vote in order to win the office, and so the system provides solutions for the instances in which this might not happen immediately (Center for Voting and Democracy [Center]). Essentially, all voters would receive a ballot on which they would rank their presidential candidate choices in order of personal preference. If after the first counting of all first choices on these ballots there is no clear majority winner, then the two top-scoring candidates are set aside and the ballots recounted. When the instance arises where a voter's first choice has been removed from the election, the system then automatically moves to her second choice on the ballot, allotting the vote to the listed candidate, if that candidate is still a part of the race. The process would continue in such a manner until a clear majority winner can be established (Center). Proponents of IRV state that among its noticed benefits would be the elimination of "the problem of spoiler candidates knocking off major candidates," the freeing of "communities of voters from splitting their vote among their own candidates," and the assurance that the election would go to "the candidate preferred by most voters" (Center).

However, IRV is not without its faults. As opponents of a popular vote are quick to point out, a presidential candidate could simply appeal to one particular majority segment of the population—such as educated, white Christians—and then carry an election while ignoring the rest of the country (Best). As Curtis Gans, Director of the Committee for the Study of the American Electorate, puts it: "While even with the Electoral College, increasingly the bulk of campaign resources are poured into televised political advertising, direct elections would insure that all monetary resources would be poured into such advertising." Essentially this argument states that candidates would no longer feel the need to actually campaign in an election. Instead, whichever side poured more money into negative political advertising and was able to make their opponent look worse would win the Presidency. This is clearly a major flaw in the system of direct popular elections and highlights the fact that a fair replacement for the Electoral College will not be found easily.

Those proponents of changing the Electoral College who do not share the view of IRV supporters that our current system should be completely abolished have come up with a solution of their own, one that they feel avoids the pitfalls commonly associated with a direct popular election. The new system would require little change in the way that the actual electoral districts and measures are laid out. However, the process of election itself would undergo a drastic retooling. This solution to the current woes of the Electoral College is known as Proportional Representation (PR), and it provides an alternative to the idea of a direct popular vote.

The principle behind a presidential election system of Proportional Representation is fairly simple and is based on a platform that has been pushed for at local and state levels for quite some time (Richie). Already adopted in the states of New Hampshire and Maine, PR would simply award electoral votes to each candidate based roughly on what percentage of the population he or she carried (Gans). Each state in the union is awarded a number of electoral votes equal to the number of its national Senators (two for every state) plus the number of their national Representatives. Rather than having this entire sum of votes awarded to whichever candidate receives a statewide majority of the popular vote, the electoral votes would be divided and then voted on. A statewide election for President—much like the ones held now—would determine which candidate receives the two votes representing the state's Senators. The remaining electoral votes would be broken down to one vote per congressional district. These votes would then be awarded based on whichever candidate won the popular vote in that particular district (Gans). Proponents of PR state that this system would "produce an electoral tally closer to the popular vote than the current statewide system," increase the clout and credibility of third-party candidates, "enhance American pluralism by making the votes of significant minorities more instrumental in the overall outcome," and seemingly increase the importance of each person's vote, thus bolstering voter confidence and turnout (Gans).

However, there are a good many people opposed to this system of presidential election. In their minds the current Electoral College has worked without a hitch for over 200 years and thus must be doing something right (Best). Also, by dividing the awarded electoral votes in a way such as PR, it is highly possible that a majority of the electoral vote—270 of the 538 possible votes—would be increasingly difficult for one candidate to secure (Best). Thus, there is the possibility of constantly turning elections over to the House of Representatives as laid out in the Constitution when a majority of the electorate is not achieved by any one person (Cummings A7). A lengthened election coupled with a President chosen by Representatives as opposed to general voters is not seen by some as a viable replacement of the current College.

As has been shown, there is definitely a problem with the Electoral College and its present-day incarnation in America. However, the alternatives to the College themselves are not perfect, and thus the process of finding a replacement for our current system of presidential election is a complicated one. There are no clear-cut answers and no definitive and easily identifiable solutions, only the knowledge—made even more apparent by recent election woes—that something not quite right exists within the Electoral College and its role in the election process. Proportional Representation and Instant Runoff Voting are the two most prominent solutions available, though there is no telling if in either lies the future of our country. An answer must be found soon, though, if the levels of pride in American democracy are to remain high. The rest of the world often turns to America and its political system for guidance in molding their own institutions, though few have ever adopted an election process similar to ours. Perhaps it is time that we as a country begin paying attention to the nations surrounding us for a change and observing the benefits and drawbacks of voting customs around the world. America may be a premier country for the institution of government itself, but it is quickly becoming painfully obvious that simply being the "American way" does not make a process credible. With hope the majority of us will notice this fact before "America the Beautiful" becomes the stuff of fairy tales.

Works Cited

Amar, Akhil. Unites States. Congress. House of Representatives Subcommittee on the Constitution of the Committee on the Judiciary. <u>Subcommittee Hearing on "Proposals for Electoral College Reform: H.J. Res.28 and H.J. Res. 43.</u>" 105th Cong., 1st session. 4 Sept. 1997. Washington, DC: GPO, 1997. 11 Nov. 2000.
<http: <u>www.house.gov/judiciary/222315.htm</u>>

Best, Judith A. Unites States. Congress. House of Representatives Subcommittee on the Constitution of the Committee on the Judiciary. <u>Subcommittee Hearing on "Proposals for Electoral College Reform: H.J. Res.28 and H.J. Res. 43.</u>" 105th Cong., 1st session. 4 Sept. 1997. Washington, DC: GPO, 1997. 11 Nov. 2000.
< <u>http://www.house.gov/judiciary/222314.htm</u>>

The Center for Voting and Democracy. "Instant Runoff Voting: A Fairer Way to Conduct Single-Winner Elections (IRV)." <u>The Center for Voting and Democracy Web Site</u>. 25 Nov. 2000. <http://www.fairvote.org/irv/a_fairer_way.htm>

Cummings, Milton C., Jr. "Public Opinion and Interest Groups." <u>Democracy Under Pressure</u>. Eighth edition. Fort Worth: Harcourt Brace College Publishers, 1997.

Gans, Curtis. Unites States. Congress. House of Representatives Subcommittee on the Constitution of the Committee on the Judiciary. <u>Subcommittee Hearing on "Proposals for Electoral College Reform: H.J. Res.28 and H.J. Res. 43.</u>" 105th Cong., 1st session. 4 Sept. 1997. Washington, DC: GPO, 1997. 11 Nov. 2000.
<<u>http://www.house.gov/judiciary/222316.htm</u>>

Richie, Rob, and Steven Hill. "The Case for Proportional Representation." <u>The Center for Voting and Democracy Web Site</u>. 23 August 2000. From "Proportional

Representation: Are Winner-Take-All Elections Fair?"
Social Policy 26.4 (1996): 25-38. 25 November 2000.
<http://www.fairvote.org/pr/progressive.htm>

Sung, Ellen. "Time to Reform the Electoral College?"
Speakout.com. 27 July 2000. 3 March 2001.
<http://www.speakout.com/Content/DailyBriefing/2733/>

The Effect of American Culture on Native Americans

By Carmela Parish

English 1102: Literary Analysis

Native Americans suffered many hardships with the arrival of the Europeans. When this country was being colonized, the natives lost physical possessions such as their land. However, in the 20th century, with the onslaught of modern culture, the natives lost things that probably meant more to them than their land. The story "Lullaby" by Leslie Marmon Silko shows us that these important things, their families and their culture, were often lost even when they tried to adapt or fit in with the American society.

The American culture destroyed for the Indians one of the most important and basic factors in their society: the family. Ayah lost her family at the hands of the "whites." Her children were taken away from her because of some disease that they had (809). In many cases like this the government had good intentions, but the emotional and mental welfare of the children and parents was not considered. Ayah shows how distraught she was by saying that not having her children with her, yet knowing that they were alive, was worse than them being dead (809). Having the children separated from the parents broke not only the bond between parent and child, but often also the bond between husband and wife. Ayah felt as though Chato somehow had betrayed her, and therefore a heavy strain was placed on their relationship (809).

Most Native Americans also lost their culture. Their culture served a fundamental role in not only distinguishing them from whites, but it also gave them pride in themselves. The whites came and forced a new and different type of culture on them. It wasn't enough for the natives to learn the ways of the "white man." Most eventually forgot their own culture and adopted the culture of the whites as their own. That is why Ayah's grandmother admonished her not to learn their language or their ways (809). She realized that doing so would jeopardize their own culture.

The natives were still mistreated even when they tried to adapt to the new ways. Chato and his son Jimmie learned English (807). Learning the language was sort of an acceptance of American culture. Yet both of these men were mistreated. Jimmie showed more of a desire to be a part of the American culture by joining the army. However, he lost his life fighting for a country that robbed him of his culture (807). Chato also showed a form of devotion to the white rancher by working hard for him for many years (810). The rancher repaid him by firing him because he was too old to work anymore (810).

This story shows us what happens when one culture forces itself on another without recognizing the other culture's right to exist also. As in the case of the Native Americans, people of the less dominant culture often lose their families and their entire culture. Although fiction, this story should help everyone to analyze the mistakes made in the past concerning people and their different beliefs. Hopefully this will help in creating a more tolerant attitude that will not destroy so many people's lives.

Work Cited

Silko, Leslie Marmon. "Lullaby." Literature and Ourselves. Ed. Gloria Henderson, Bill Day, and Sandra Waller. Second ed. NY: Addison-Wesley, 1997. 806-13.

PRELIMINARY OR WORKING OUTLINE
The Effect of American Culture on Native Americans

I. Introduction
Thesis- The story "Lullaby" by Leslie Marmon Silko shows us that these important things, their families and their culture, were often lost even when they tried to adapt or fit in with the American society.

II. The American culture destroyed for the Indians one of the most important and basic factors in their society: the family.
        A. Supporting Point: Families were broken apart by the government.
        B. Reference to story: The government took Ayah's children, which caused a strain on her relationship with Chato.
III. Most Native Americans also lost their culture.
        A. Supporting Point: The American culture invaded the lives of the natives and soon took over their original culture.
        B. Reference to story: Ayah's grandmother admonished her that learning the ways of the whites endangered them.
IV. The natives were still mistreated even when they tried to adapt to the new ways.
        A. Supporting Point: Trying to become more like the Americans was sometimes more destructive than resisting.
        B. Reference to story: Jimmie died fighting for this country, and Chato was fired after years of hard work.
 V. Conclusion
        A. Review: The natives lost their families and their culture.
        B. Conclusion: Examining the past may help us to become more tolerant.

A Mother's Education

By Cora McCray

English 1102: Literary Analysis

In everyday life, people affect those around them in either a positive or negative manner, whether purposefully or by accident. With some, it is known from birth or youth that they will change someone's life. It is not as if these people bear a special symbol or do things in a certain manner; it is just the way they are. In "Everyday Use," by Alice Walker, the narrator's daughter Dee is an example of how one person brings about change in another just by being herself. Throughout the story, Dee's growing education and confidence maker her mother bold and confident.

While Dee was young and growing up in her mother's house, her mother knew Dee was different from the other children in the area. Also, Dee felt she was above her mother and sister. This attitude was apparent to Dee's mother as early as grade school, when she says that Dee "used to read to [. . .] us two, sitting trapped and ignorant underneath her voice" (1086-7). Dee hated the way she lived as a child and "wanted nice things" (1087), things her mother was unable to give her due to the family's financial situation. In the beginning of the story, Dee's mother is reflecting on her life and making comparisons between herself and her daughter. The pride Dee's mother has for her daughter and the education Dee is getting is apparent when the mother remarks, "I never had an education myself" (1087). The mother, while awaiting Dee's arrival, also looks at her surroundings in the way she knows Dee will. Dee's mother deliberately turns her back on her house, because she knows Dee is ashamed of it (1087). Even though Dee was a child, her mother still took Dee's thoughts and opinions to heart because Dee was always important and special to her.

When Dee comes to visit her mother and sister, she has thoroughly embraced the ideals and awareness associated with Black heritage which had a resurgence in the 1960's. Dee has changed her name to something her mother has difficulty pronouncing because she says she "'couldn't bear it any longer, being named after the people who oppress me'" (1088). Dee's mother, because she has little time or desire to keep up with current events and only knows what she has lived with all her life, does not feel that Dee's name is any sign of oppression because she was named for a relative. With Dee's new emergence of self-awareness, the house that Dee resented all of her childhood now becomes a source of fascination for her because it holds so many things that made her who she is. For instance, upon Dee's arrival, she takes many pictures, "making sure the house is included" (1088). She also asks her mother for the butter churn and several quilts. These things are not only just physical expressions of her childhood and the way she was raised, but these items become emblems of who she wants to be. However, Dee does not want these things because they hold any emotional value for her; she only wants them so she can have something tangible to show her friends of her true identity and heritage. She even scoffs at the idea of the quilts being given to her sister, Maggie, who is "'backward enough to put them to everyday use'" (1091). It is apparent that Dee's self-awareness does not include an appreciation for the family structure.

Therefore, as Dee argues for the quilts and Maggie says Dee can have them, the change in Dee's mother becomes obvious. Dee's mother thinks Maggie gives up the quilts "like somebody used to never winning anything, or having anything reserved for her" (1091), and she realizes that despite Dee's education and new attitude, Dee is not better than she is or better than Maggie. This realization causes her to do some things she "never had done before" (1091). For the first time, the mother does not acquiesce to Dee's whims or desires. This discussion over the quilts helps Dee's mother to stand her ground with Dee, especially since she had offered Dee the same quilts earlier, but Dee had refused them. Dee's confidence in her new identity is mirrored by her mother's confidence in her dealings with Dee. The mother stands up to Dee and argues in favor of Maggie, something she had never done before.

In conclusion, Dee's visit changes her mother in ways that can never be reversed. While she is proud of Dee because of her education, her mother also realizes that Dee does not have to be treated as if she is better than her own mother or sister Maggie. Although Dee is very important to her mother, the mother no longer allows Dee to rule her life by giving in to Dee's desires. When Dee went home to visit her mother and sister, she did not consider that her mother's view of her would change or that her mother would be affected at all, but that is what happened. Although Dee did not set out to change her mother's life, the result is a mother emboldened and confident in the way she has lived and continues to live her life.

Work Cited

Walker, Alice. "Everyday Use." Literature and Ourselves. Ed. Gloria Henderson, Bill Day, and Sandra Waller. Second ed. NY: Addison-Wesley, 1997. 1085-92.

Dignity in Death: Frost's "The Death of the Hired Man"

By Paula Clay

English 1102: Literary Analysis with one secondary source

Robert Frost's poem "The Death of the Hired Man" illustrates the use of symbolism and diction to set the tone for a story about death and dignity. The characters are Mary, a warm and loving wife; Warren, a stern and callused husband; and Silas, a weary hired hand. Mary and Warren are dynamic, believable, and consistent characters portrayed by the dialogue expressed within the poem. Silas is a static character described by the dialogue of the other characters. The theme of the poem is interpersonal relationships and how people view the sum of an individual's life contributions. Edward Garnett contends that, in "The Death of a Hired Man," Frost portrays "a dramatic dialogue characterized by an exquisite precision of psychological insight" (492).

Mary is a loving and compassionate wife who attempts to show respect for and trust in others. Mary, having always recognized Silas's personal worth, continues to be her "brother's keeper" now that Silas's end is near. The moon symbolizes Mary's shining brightness, insight, and kindheartedness toward Silas in lines 103 through 110:

> Part of the moon was falling down to the west,
> Dragging the whole sky with it to the hills.
> Its light poured softly in her lap. She saw it
> And spread her apron to it. She put out her hand
> Among the harplike morning-glory strings
> Taunt with the dew from garden bed to eaves,
> As if she played unheard some tenderness
> That wrought on him beside her in the night.

Mary consistently plays the role of peacemaker between Silas and Warren by expressing compassion for Silas's situation in lines 49 and 50: "Surely you wouldn't grudge the poor old man / Some humble way to save his self-respect." Mary recognizes Silas's situation and is protective of his dignity and respect as he is dying.

In contrast to his wife, Warren is cold, stern, and rigid in expressing his feelings about Silas. Warren views his relationship with Silas as strictly functional; he values Silas only for his utility as a farm worker. Warren remains emotionally distant about their relationship as evident in lines 13 through 17:

> I told him so last haying, didn't I?
> If he left then, I said, that ended it.
> What good is he? Who else will harbor him
> At his age for the little he can do?
> What help he is there's no depending on.

Warren fails to recognize the significance of Silas's choice to return to die in their home, instead of his own brother's. Warren prefers to break off the relationship with Silas, now that he offers little value as a worker. This attitude is symbolized in lines 122 and 123, "Picked up a little stick, and brought it back / And broke it in his hand and tossed it by."

Silas considers the most significant talent in his life to be his knack for bailing hay. That Mary perceives this is evidenced in lines 88 and 89: "I know, that's Silas' one accomplishment / He bundles every forkful in its place." Silas wishes to pass on his talent to someone else, so as to leave something of himself in this world: "He thinks if he could teach him that, he'd be / Some good perhaps to someone in the world" (96-97). The little silver cloud that "hits the moon" near the end of the poem symbolizes Silas's death in lines 162 to 164:

> It hit the moon.
> Then there were three there, making a dim row,
> The moon, the silver cloud, and she.

The value of our achievements is relative to our life experiences. Silas valued his achievements and the quality of life differently than Warren. Warren measured the value of a man over a span of time and the total sum of material worth, while Silas valued life simply by one single task. Frost's poem forces us to reflect on how we view the sum of our accomplishments. Will our own view be more important than the viewpoint of others? How we judge the value of a person's life is influenced by our own unique life experiences. Succinctly stated, Frost provides insight on the importance of treating people facing imminent death with dignity and respect, and since there is a tendency to internalize the value of our achievements at the time of our deaths, helping others to remain cognizant of their self-worth provides them with a sense of a life well-lived, a goal we all surely share.

Works Cited

Frost, Robert. "Death of a Hired Man." The Poetry of Robert Frost. Ed. Edward Connery Lathem. NY: Holt, 1928. Rpt. Literature and Ourselves. Eds. Gloria Henderson, Brian Day, and Sandra Waller. Third ed. NY: Addison-Wesley, 2000. 483-88.

Garnett, Edward. "A New American Poet." Atlantic Monthly August 1915. Rpt. Literature and Ourselves. Eds. Gloria Henderson, Brian Day, and Sandra Waller. Third ed. NY: Addison-Wesley, 2000. 491-92.

Taking a Life in Order to Live Their Way of Life

By Santina Bennett

English 1102: Literary Analysis

What are some of the effects experienced by a young couple when their relationship has to deal with an unwanted pregnancy? Can their bond overcome the turmoil of having to make the decision between the giving of life or having an abortion? In Ernest Hemingway's "Hills Like White Elephants," the reader is given a peek at how the frivolous lifestyle of a couple is jarred and their puerile relationship is torn apart when they are confronted with an unwanted pregnancy. The conflict of opinion between them, of either bringing their unborn child into the world or having an abortion to end its life, brings them deep confusion. The reader is witness to their selfish immaturity and their resentment at having to possibly change their lifestyle in order to face the responsibility of bringing the product of their union into the world. And in the end the couple's strong difference of opinion on how to resolve this life-changing matter between them brings to them the ultimate realization that no matter what their final choice is, their lives and relationship will never be the same.

The narrator lets the reader eavesdrop on a traveling couple's conversation. They are sitting at a bar near a train station in Ebro, Spain, waiting for the express to Madrid (323). While the couple patiently waits, they go through several drinks each and seem to be in a heated conversation about a simple operation (323-24). The man is a rich, arrogant, and controlling American who is trying to convince the woman he impregnated that the unmentionable abortion he wants her to have is simple, easy, and natural. "'It's really an awfully simple operation, Jig [. . .]. It's not really an operation at all'" (324). He is very insistent and tries to convince Jig that the only way they will be happy again is to

117

have this simple operation. Not convinced that an abortion would place them on the road to happiness, Jig questions his reasoning. He responds: "'That's the only thing that bothers us. It's the only thing that's made us unhappy'" (324). He shows a callous, pompous, and irresponsible attitude about his unborn child; he is more concerned with his carefree lifestyle being disrupted than the fact that he will be taking a life in order to live his life in the manner to which he has become accustomed.

Jig, on the other hand, seems a bit more concerned than the American about making such a momentous decision. As she gazes at the different landscapes along the banks of the Ebro, she correlates the rich fields of grain and the lovely hills of one region to the barren, sun-burned expanse of the other side. Her metaphors of fertility as the child within her and the barrenness as abortion deeply stir her emotions and add to her confusion over what to do (325). In an effort to have the American understand her dilemma, she tries to convince him that they can have a good, fruitful, rich life even if they keep their child: "'And we could have all this,' she said. 'And we could have everything and every day we make it more impossible'" (325). She shows a hint of fear in making a wrong decision and winding up with nothing: "'And once they take it away, you never get it back'" (325).

At the onset of this story, Jig refers to the white hills as white elephants (323). The white elephants (that is, unwanted, discarded items) are used as symbolism of Jig's unwanted, unborn fetus. After much soul searching and deep contemplation, she later sees the hills in their true beauty: "'They're lovely hills. They don't really look like white elephants'" (324). The life she is leading does not seem as fun and fulfilling any more. When sipping a new drink, she makes the statement that it is all the same, "'It tastes like licorice [. . .]. Everything tastes of licorice. Especially all the things you've waited so long for, like absinthe'" (323-24). She further states, "'That's all we do, isn't it—look at things and try new drinks?'" (324). She is definitely disenchanted with living the fast life and is desperately trying to grow and mature by making a responsible decision, but her partner in life will not hear of it. In his single-mindedness, he feels the only way back to a pleasant, carefree lifestyle is to have this simple operation. He continues to try and convince her how easy it will be: "'I know you wouldn't mind it, Jig. It's really not anything. It's just to let the air in'" (324).

In the end Jig realizes she cannot convince her man to keep their child. She is still very immature and needy and is desperate for his love and attention. He tries to reassure her of his love and insists he will go along with her final decision, but Jig can see beyond that and realizes that he wants his own way (324). She asks in desperation, "'And if I do it you'll be happy and things will be like they were and you'll love me?'" (324). He claims to love her and that he will always love her and states that he only wants her in his life (324-25). Inside her womb rests the result of their union. Can their relationship ever be the same if they have to take their child's life in order to continue to live their lives? Can love and happiness exist between the two of them if they abort their child? Jig realizes that things will never be the same between the two of them: "'Do you feel better?' he asked. 'I feel fine,' she said. 'There's nothing wrong with me. I feel fine'" (326). Unfortunately, she is not strong or mature enough to stand by her beliefs and convictions, so she allows herself to be manipulated and controlled by someone who professes to love her.

Work Cited

Hemingway, Ernest. "Hills Like White Elephants." Literature and Ourselves: A Thematic Introduction for Readers and Writers. Ed. Gloria Henderson, Bill Day and Sandra Waller. Second edition. New York: Addison-Wesley, 1997. 322-327.

Sex, Violence and Religion?: John Donne's Holy Sonnet XIV

By Susan Fleming

English 1102: Literary Analysis, Researched

When taking a closer look at John Donne's Holy Sonnet XIV, one notices that it reveals more about the relationship that Donne desired to have with God. In this sonnet, a theme of violence and sexual conquest is present. The speaker is asking God to violently possess him. God is in the role of the male aggressor, while the speaker is in the traditional, subordinate female role. In describing the opening and closing lines of the poem, Richard Steir declares, "They rely on the conception of total spiritual dependence on God, on the need for man to be utterly regenerated by God, not merely aided and assisted by him" (375). The poem opens by the speaker asking the "three-personed God" to "batter my heart" (line 1). "Three-personed" is referring to the Trinity--Father, Son, and Holy Ghost. The word "heart" in Donne's time had a sexual connotation, according to Craig Payne, "'heart' also being Elizabethan slang for the vagina" (211). This is to foreshadow much of the imagery of the poem. The speaker is asking God to "knock, breathe, shine" (2) in order to make him new.

Line four seems to be a metaphor, comparing the speaker to some type of malleable metal, perhaps gold, using "force to break, blow, burn, and make me new," like one would heat metal to make it soft enough to shape and mold it until the metal became what one wanted it to be. To some extent, the speaker seems to be playing hard to get. He wants to be taken by God, yet his defenses are strong. The image of an "usurped town" in line 5 reveals this fact. Like a town that is being held under siege, the speaker has his defenses up. Just as a town must be won over by force in most cases, so must the speaker. However, a town is usually not as

120

strong as it appears to be from the outside. This can be compared to when the speaker describes his defenses as "weak or untrue" in line 8. The speaker utters his love for God in line 9, but shortly after, a complication arises. The speaker explains that he is "betrothed unto your enemy" (10). The "enemy" seems to refer to Satan and his sinful nature. Like someone trapped in a bad marriage, he must be divorced from Satan. He begs God to "[d]ivorce me, untie or break that knot again" (11), because he cannot break away alone.

In order for him to be free from his sinful ways, he calls God to violence. The poem states, "Take me to You, imprison me [. . .]" (12). In the most shocking request of all, the speaker asks God to ravish him so that he can be free and chaste. It is the act of being ravished, or raped, that will free him from his sin. Payne says that the rape can be interpreted to be spiritual:

> That which is humanly imperfect and even exploitative becomes divinely perfect and fulfilling. The rape preserves, rather than destroys, chastity. God builds up as He tears down, possesses as He frees. (212)

While man may try to escape from God, he is naturally drawn to Him. A human's imperfections are part of God's design, so that one must draw closer to Him and depend upon Him.

Looking at the sonnet in terms of Donne's own life, one sees him drawn towards God but caught in conflict. He realizes his own limitations, that he is sinful by nature, yet he desperately needs God in his life. In the sonnet, he is asking God to take control of his life. He feels separated from God because of his shortcomings. Steir states that Donne could not see himself as free from sin:

> Donne finds it difficult to accept being saved as a sinner and he cannot convincingly imagine being free from sin. In the absence of the capacity to imagine or feel either of these, Donne's deepest prayer must be either to be ravished into chastity, or to escape from God's attention. (384)

Donne wanted God to intervene directly in his life and bring Donne closer to Him. Donne could not bring himself directly to God because he felt that he was unworthy. He believed that his sinful past kept him from having the closeness with God that he desired.

It was once thought that the collection of "Holy Sonnets" was composed after Donne had become an Anglican preacher. However, later this was found not to be the case. The sonnets were composed when Donne was in deep despair. As R. C. Bald notes, "These sonnets were not written, as was earlier supposed, by a man in holy orders, but during a period of Donne's life when he had no vocation and felt keenly that he had no place in the divinely ordered scheme" (236). A lack of specific religious faith at this time in his life disturbed him. He had abandoned the Catholic faith, the only faith he had ever known, so he could marry his love. But he was reluctant to turn to a Protestant religion. Without religion, there was a void in Donne's life.

A closer examination of some of the other "Holy Sonnets" reveals more intimately the details of Donne's religious conflict. He was uncertain of what death would bring and feared it deeply. An eternity of hell terrified him, but the path to heaven was uncertain to him. Because of this fear, Donne attempted to domesticate death as much as possible by considering every aspect of it. To neutralize and rechannel his fears, he had to write on and preach on. He had to convince himself that death would not separate him from the one thing he longed to be so close to. The "Holy Sonnets" are a poetic record of Donne's intense struggle with God and death.

Works Cited

Bald, R. C. <u>John Donne: A Life</u>. NY: Oxford UP, 1970.

Donne, John. "Holy Sonnet 14." <u>Literature: An Introduction to Reading and Writing</u>. Ed. Edgar V. Roberts and Henry E. Jacobs. Compact edition. Upper Saddle River, NJ: Prentice-Hall, 1998. 479.

Payne, Craig. "Donne's Holy Sonnet XIV." <u>The Explicator</u> 54.4 (1996): 211-12.

Steir, Richard. "John Donne Awry and Squint: The 'Holy Sonnets,' 1608-1610." <u>Modern Philology</u> 86.4 (1989): 375-84.

The story of Oedipus, that he would kill his father and marry his mother, has been popular among people of every generation. It is such a captivating story that many great writers have tried to transform it from mere words to classic drama. However, of all the writers who have tried to capture Oedipus' story, none were as successful as Sophocles. When people think of Oedipus, they usually think of Sophocles' rendition of his story. Some think Sophocles' success is because of the peculiar content of the story, and others think it is because of how he approached the subject. I think Sophocles' success lies largely in his method of characterization. By showing us the personalities of the characters in the play instead of telling us their traits, Sophocles allowed us to know more about the characters than he could have ever told us. In the play *Oedipus the King*, Sophocles presents Oedipus as a tragic hero because he, through his own actions, revitalizes the city of Thebes and brings about his own demise in the process.

By Aristotle's definition, Oedipus is a perfect example of what a tragic hero should be. In the Prologue we learn that Oedipus has great respect and admiration in Thebes. He has an outstanding reputation as a savior of Thebes because he solved the Sphinx's riddle and rescued the people from its terror. This deed satisfies one of Aristotle's requirements of a tragic hero—that he must be highly renowned. However, by solving the Sphinx's riddle, Oedipus not only gained respect and admiration, but also a new life filled with prosperity. After solving the Sphinx's riddle, Oedipus is pronounced king of Thebes, a position that also allowed him to marry the queen, Jocasta. The extensive prosperity that he gains after solving the riddle satisfies Aristotle's second requirement of a tragic hero—that he must be prosperous. Finally, Oedipus' own actions satisfy a third requirement of a tragic hero—that his misfortune must be brought about by some error or frailty. When Oedipus declares to the people of Thebes that he will find the man who killed Laius and send him away to live out his life in exile, he does not know that he is laying a curse upon himself (251-253). Oedipus' error was overzealously committing himself to a punishment when he did not know who was being punished. By satisfying Aristotle's requirements of a tragic hero, Oedipus is automatically expected to endure severe misfortune because of his own actions.

In the play, the first of three questions that Oedipus must answer in order to uncover who killed Laius is: who is the murderer? Oedipus feels that because he succeeded Laius as king of Thebes, it is his responsibility to find Laius' murderer. He also feels that because of his talent for solving riddles, he is superbly capable of finding the man who killed Laius. Therefore, Oedipus begins to pursue the answer to this question by the easiest and most obvious path, which is through a prophet, Tiresias. Tiresias is hesitant to tell Oedipus who Laius' murderer is because he knows it is Oedipus, and he would rather have Oedipus destroy himself by finding out the truth his own way, which would also be the only way he would believe it. When Oedipus accuses Tiresias of talking stupidly and being somehow involved in Laius' death, Tiresias, in an angry rage, tells Oedipus that his real parents did not think he was a fool. Then Oedipus, remembering the oracle's prophecy from so long ago, begins to question his own identity and credibility. The Theban elders, with continued confidence in Oedipus and his innocence, point out that although Tiresias is a prophet, he is still a mortal capable of making mistakes (Segal 109). Oedipus also does not believe that he killed Laius; however, now that there is a question of his birth, Oedipus begins to remember the circumstances under which he came to Thebes. By questioning his birth, Oedipus begins to realize that the prophecy he tried to prevent from coming true may have already been fulfilled. Instead of finding the answer to his original question of who the murderer is, Oedipus is led to a second question: am I the murderer? The investigation of Laius' murder has already gone off course, and Oedipus' downfall has begun.

Following the path that his investigation has taken, Oedipus questions Jocasta about specific details surrounding Laius' death and is "suddenly struck with the almost certain suspicion that, unawares, he has committed a terrible murder" (Cameron 47). Needing more proof than mere suspicion, he tells Jocasta to send for the herdsman who she says relayed the story of Laius' death to her. However, before the herdsman arrives, a messenger from Corinth, the place where Oedipus was raised, came to report to Oedipus that Polybus was dead and the people of Corinth had named Oedipus king. Oedipus and the people of Thebes prematurely rejoice that Oedipus is innocent, that he did not kill his father whom most people believed was King Polybus of Corinth. Jocasta tells Oedipus not to worry anymore because no one could truly foresee the future. Both Oedipus and Jocasta were wrong in their assumptions. The messenger from Corinth informed Oedipus that Polybus was not his biological father, but that a stranger who left him with the king and queen to be raised as their own had brought him to Corinth. Not only does this information halt Oedipus' celebration of innocence, but it also raises a question that has lingered in Oedipus' mind since the oracle's prophecy. The question that he has yet to find an answer to is: who am I? At this point in the play, the plague that was originally the cause of the grand investigation of Laius' murder has become almost insignificant. The people of Thebes wait patiently for an end to their grief while "Oedipus's search for his origins completely overshadows the sufferings of the city" (Segal 72).

The herdsman who witnessed Laius' death is the only person who can solve the mysteries of Oedipus' birth and Laius' murder, but he also is hesitant to tell Oedipus anything that he knows. When Oedipus threatens to torture the herdsman until he tells him what he knows about the baby he was ordered to kill, it shows us that Oedipus is willing to do whatever is necessary to find out where he was born and who his true parents are. Oedipus feels that he would be less of a man if he did not seek out the truth about his birth after coming so far and being so close to knowing the truth (1063-1064). Finally, the herdsman admits that he was ordered to kill a child that was rumored to be Laius' son because the oracle had prophesied that the child would kill his parents. Oedipus is overwhelmed with disgust and horror when he realizes that the child who had been spared by the herdsman was him. Oedipus' surge of emotions is triggered by his recognition that the prophecy that had been told to his parents had come true and that no one could have stopped the prophecy from becoming truth. Oedipus finally gets the answers to the three questions presented to him throughout the play. He knows that he is the murderer and that Laius was his father.

Once Oedipus recognizes that the oracle's prophecy had come true, he retreats into the palace to find his wife and mother dead. Jocasta commits suicide when she realizes that the horrid event that she tried to prevent had occurred anyway. When Oedipus sees his wife hanging there dead, he blinds himself, unwilling to see the world he has created. Oedipus understood that he had brought himself misery by blindly pursuing a case that many begged him not to ("Oedipus"). He felt that after all the misery that he had brought to the people around him, he no longer deserved to see the beauty and pleasantness of the world.

When Oedipus is brought outside by a servant for the people of Thebes to see what he has done, he is a completely different person from the Oedipus that reigned as king of Thebes. Oedipus has become a man full of self-hatred. When he comes out, he curses the man who "freed the savage shackles from [his] feet...and became [his] savior" (1359-1365). Oedipus believes that if he had died as a child instead of being allowed to live a full life, he would not have been able to cause the pain and grief to himself, his family, or the people of Thebes. Oedipus has become a plague not only to the city, but also to himself and everyone that has come in contact with him. Everyone who was close to him was somehow stained by the truth of Oedipus' fate. His wife was the mother and grandmother to his children; his children had to live with the shame of knowing they were the result of an incestuous mother-son relationship; the people of Thebes suffered an intense plague because they failed to seek out the killer of their previous king.

Some people would argue that Oedipus' tragic downfall was based solely on the nature of the events in his life, but many different things caused Oedipus' downfall. If Oedipus had been a middle-class citizen of Thebes, his story would not have been so tragic because his life would not have affected the entire city. If Oedipus had been evil and merciless as ruler of Thebes, the citizens would not have cared because they would have been happy to rid themselves of such vileness. However, because of his unblemished reputation as savior and king of Thebes, Oedipus' downfall affected everyone in the city to an unimaginable extent. The people of Thebes were both happy to know that they would be saved from the plague and sad to know that they would lose a great king. By finally discovering that he is the plague causing Thebes so much anguish and punishing himself with his self-inflicted blindness, Oedipus not only releases the people of Thebes from their grief, but also causes his immediate downfall because one can not exist without the other. If Oedipus had not punished himself, Thebes would have continued to suffer from the plague and eventually be destroyed by it, but Oedipus would have retained his unblemished reputation among the people of Thebes. Oedipus is a true tragic hero because through all of his stubbornness, he still managed to revitalize the city of Thebes, even though it meant that his life had to come to the unfortunate end of losing everything that he loved, including the person he thought was his true self.

The story of Oedipus, that he would kill his father and marry his mother, has intrigued many from the time of the ancient Greeks to the present day. Despite its popularity and the many interpretations of it, no one can tell exactly why Oedipus' story has managed to be universally read and loved throughout time. However, most readers agree that he is a tragic hero because he revitalizes the city of Thebes and brings about his own demise in the process. During his struggle to rid Thebes of the man who plagues it, he is confronted with three questions: who is the murderer? am I the murderer? who am I? The answers to these questions successfully provide the citizens of Thebes with a solution to all their problems, but bring more problems to Oedipus. However, Oedipus fights blindly for what he feels is right. He searches for an answer to rid Thebes of its plague and himself of the curiosity of his origins. Some people argue that Oedipus deserves everything that comes to him because Apollo warned him of his doom, but he fulfills it through his own actions (Jevons 61). Of everyone that reads Oedipus' story, I believe that only a few feel this way.

Works Cited

Aristotle. "Poetics." Trans. S. H. Butcher. 2000. The Internet
   Classics Archive. 19 November 2000.
   <http://classics.mit.edu//Aristotle/poetics.html>.

Cameron, Alister. The Identity of Oedipus the King: Five Essays
   on the Oedipus Tyrannus. New York: New York
   University Press, 1968.

Jevons, Frank B. "In Sophoclean Tragedy, Humans Create Their
   Own Fate." Readings on Sophocles. San Diego:
   Greenhaven Press, 1997. 59-62.

"Oedipus Rex: Classic Tragic Hero." Mrs. Jordan's Class Page. 18
   November 2000.
   <http://www.geocities.com/rainforest/canopy/8108/oedipus
   2.html>.

Segal, Charles. Oedipus Tyrannus: Tragic Heroism and the Limits
   of Knowledge. New York: Twayne Publishers, 1993.

Sophocles. "Oedipus the King." Trans. Thomas Gould. Literature
   and Ourselves. Ed. Gloria Henderson, Bill Day, and
   Sandra Waller. 2nd ed. New York: Addison-Wesley,
   1997. 1237-1277.

Deconstructing Jocasta

By Linda Rosenbaum

English 1102: Literary Analysis, Researched; Comparison/Contrast

There are a few theories about Jocasta, the Queen of Thebes, but there is no definitive profile of her. I wonder how Sophocles, in writing *Oedipus the King*, intended for Jocasta to be perceived? She is only present on the stage for a brief time, but she has a large and pivotal role for a woman in the fifth century B. C. She is aristocratic and mysterious, and I believe she endures the most shame of any character. It is difficult to capture a complete sense of what Jocasta really knows or what she is responsible for. She behaves as one might expect royalty to behave, and she displays a caring and fair nature. Jocasta is somewhat reserved, so the reader learns more about her through her actions than what she says. When Jocasta first appears in Sophocles' play during an argument between Oedipus and Creon, the reader sees her as a peacemaker, a sensible wife and sister, the voice of reason and a fair judge.

In two stylistically different films (both entitled *Oedipus Rex*) based on the play, the two actresses who portray Jocasta are very different. The more recent of the two films was originally released in 1967 and was written and directed by the Italian director Pier Paolo Pasolini. Pasolini's Jocasta is portrayed by the elegant Silvana Mangano who, according to *The World Encyclopedia of the Film,* is the wife of Italian film producer Dino de Laurentiis and a former dancer. This Jocasta is beautiful, youthful, statuesque and extremely pale with finely chiseled features. She is an enigma seen frolicking gaily with several maiden attendants, waving incense with symbols of prayer and supplication (to seek guidance from the gods) in one scene, and hanging by a rope, dead by her own hand moments later.

The 1957 version of *Oedipus Rex* is more faithful to the play. The dialogue was written by the Nobel laureate William Butler Yeats and is comparable to the Thomas Gould translation in the textbook *Literature and Ourselves*. It is actually a filmed play done in the classic style of Sophocles' day. All of the actors wear masks. The mask Oedipus wears gives him a noble look with a somewhat pained expression, while Jocasta's mask is particularly grotesque. They both wear long, awful, claw-like gloves. This Jocasta is performed by Eleanor Stuart. Since she dons a mask, the audience sees only one expression, but her voice is clearly the voice of an older woman. She is mercurial, for she is seen to change her mood and tone very quickly. She is self-assured with a commanding voice, seeming dignified but not reserved.

Jocasta tries to manipulate Oedipus by pretending not to believe in the prophecy told about him, but she appeals to the gods when she feels threatened. In an effort to calm the excitable Oedipus, she claims, "no mortal is ever given skill in prophecy" (713-714). This statement is clearly to deter Oedipus from pursuing any further proof of the prophecy. She is already becoming fearful of the unspeakable outcome of this pursuit of the truth when she says to Oedipus, "True foresight isn't possible. His life is best who lives without a plan" (983-984).

At times Jocasta seems to have blind faith in the prophecies. Even though she appears to change her mind about those beliefs depending upon the situation, in the end when it matters to her most, she counts on the prophets to lead her to the right path. Jocasta realized the critical nature of the recollection of the servant who survived the attack in which Laius lost his life. She responds to Oedipus' summoning the servant, "He can't reject that and reverse himself. The city heard these things, not I alone" (854-855). Also in the same episode, when Jocasta prays to the "Lords of the realm" (916), it is obvious that it is inherent in her to believe the prophecies, and she is becoming so desperate that she appeals to Apollo for answers. But there is no stopping the awful truth from surfacing. Anthony Boyer writes in "The Classics Pages" that Jocasta tested the beliefs of those around her by feigning disbelief in the gods herself. He claims that though she put up this false front, she did keep her faith. It was an accepted practice to believe in the gods at that time. How else could Jocasta live with the fact that she and her husband set out to kill their only child in an attempt to reverse their fate as told by the prophet?

In Episode 2, Jocasta seems to put the blame of believing the oracle's prophecy solely on Laius when she says,

> That time Apollo did not make our child
> A patricide, or bring about what Laius
> Feared, that he be killed by his own son.
> That's how prophetic words determined things?
>
> (725-728)

Also in that statement, Jocasta takes a passive stance when she implicates Laius in the killing of their son. Pasolini too puts all of the blame on Laius for sending Oedipus away to die. There is clear distrust and jealousy from father to son in the 1967 movie when the father says to the newborn (subtitles translated from Italian),

> You are here to take my place in the world,
> And trust me into the void,
> And rob me of all I possess.
> The first thing you will steal from me will be her.
> In fact you are already robbing me of her affections.

It is ironic just how accurate Pasolini's Laius was on all points. I wonder if Laius was better off not knowing who killed him. He died thinking that he had defeated fate. Yet the moral of this story is clearly that one can never prevent one's destiny. I believe that subconsciously, Jocasta knows Oedipus is her son who was cast out so many years ago. But what lonely widow could deny a dashing young hero who has saved her beloved city? Like Oedipus, Jocasta is arrogant enough to assume she would never fall from grace.

Today we believe one of the greater sins committed in the story is the attempt on the baby's life. It is also an act of supreme arrogance to try to cheat one's fate by killing a defenseless child. Ed Friedlander claims in *Enjoying "Oedipus the King" by Sophocles*, that in those days "it was usual to leave an unwanted or defective baby in the wilderness" (1). If that is the case, and I do not doubt it, the question remains, why did they pierce his feet and bind them? Was this added insurance that the baby would perish?

A high school English teacher in New York City has created a study guide to the play called, "Sophocles' Oedipus Tyrannus: A Map of the Soul." Ms. B. Wu says that there are no villains, only a mistake caused by the limits of human understanding. She does not deny that the killing "where three roads meet" was the one act of wrongdoing that could be called the source of all the "ills." But what must she think about the attempt of Laius and Jocasta to murder their only son? Would they be absolved of punishment because the child lived?

I feel that Oedipus wants to be a symbol and a martyr. He will march around the countryside suffering openly for all to see him. In this way he can pay for his sins, but Jocasta cannot bear to go on living with the same knowledge. She would be seen as the perpetrator in this case, since she is much older and the parent. In *Women's Voices: Quotations from Women*, the revolutionary Modern Dance performer and choreographer Martha Graham said, "All things I do are in every woman [. . .]. Every woman is Jocasta. There comes a time when a woman is a mother to her husband." Martha Graham obviously forgives Jocasta and feels a strong kinship with her. I agree that there are times when a woman "mothers" her husband, but I think there are times when a man is like a father to his wife as well. Jan Haag writes in the feminist poem "Death" that Oedipus, like all men, "is addicted to anguish" (9) and blinds himself so that he can continue to suffer. In the poem "Blindness," Haag blames the "blindness" of western civilization on Oedipus. I question the validity of that broad statement, keeping in mind that this feminist poet seems to be rather melodramatic and angry.

Some people have a clear sense of their own destiny; many do not. On Thanksgiving Day, 2000, Ernie Suggs wrote an article titled "Nourishing a Legacy" for the *Atlanta Journal-Constitution* about Elizabeth Williams Omilami. Ms. Omilami is a daughter of the late Civil Rights activist Hosea Williams, who was buried earlier that week after succumbing to cancer. Ms. Omilami is taking over for her father to help feed the hungry and homeless during the holidays as Hosea did for three decades. Regarding her new position, Ms. Omilami tells her young daughter, "You don't have a choice when it comes to your destiny. This is my destiny right now." Most people agree that the moral of *Oedipus the King* is that one cannot escape one's destiny. Some people may say it is not to seek answers from fortune-tellers. I think the moral can be augmented to say it is to accept one's fate while living life, and to participate actively and responsibly on the road to one's destiny.

Works Cited

Boyer, Anthony. "The Classics Pages." Jocasta the Pawn: a look at the role of Jocasta in Sophocles' "Oedipus Rex." Online. Internet. 2 November 2000.
<http://www.users.globalnet.co.uk/~loxias/jocasta.htm>

Friedlander, Ed. Enjoying "Oedipus the King," by Sophocles. Online. Internet. 15 November 2000.
<http://www.pathguy.comoedipus.htm>

Graham, Martha. Women's Voices: Quotations from Women. Quote. Online. Internet. 6 November 2000.
<http://www.womenshistory.about.com/homework/womenshistory/library/qu/blugram.htm?once+true& >

Haag, Jan. "Blindness" and "Death." The Jocasta Poems from The Feminist's Poems. Poetry. Online. Internet. 15 November 2000
<http://www.students.washington.edu/jhaag/Pofromjo17.html>

Oedipus Rex. Film. Dir. Tyrone Guthrie. Trans. William Butler Yeats. Dist. Corinth Films, 1957.

Oedipus Rex. Film. Dir. And Trans. Pier Paolo Pasolini, 1967.

Smith, John M. and Cawkwell, Tim, eds. The World Encyclopedia of the Film. London, England: AS&W Visual Library, 1972.

Sophocles. "Oedipus the King." Trans. Thomas Gould. <u>Literature and Ourselves</u>. Ed. Gloria Henderson, Bill Day and Sandra Waller. Second edition. New York: Addison-Wesley Longman, 1997. 1237-77.

Suggs, Ernie. "Nourishing a Legacy." <u>Atlanta Journal-Constitution</u>. 23 November 2000: E-1, 7.

Wu, Ms. B. "Sophocles' Oedipus Tyrannus: A Map of the Soul." Online. Internet. 30 October 2000. <<u>http://www.litlives.com/oedipus.html</u>>

The greatly anticipated 1962 release of Robert Mulligan's *To Kill a Mockingbird* captures the heart of the American film audience by presenting visually Harper Lee's Pulitzer Prize-winning novel of the same name. We are introduced to a sleepy southern town in the midst of the Depression during one of its most memorable events: a black man on trial for raping a white woman. We also meet Jem and Scout, the two motherless children of Atticus Finch, a prominent figure of the town and the attorney representing the man accused of rape, Tom Robinson. The power of the hand to create and to destroy is portrayed through a close-up shot in the credit sequence as Scout opens the cigar box to reveal its treasures. Using a crayon, she shades in the title of the movie and draws a mockingbird. Then, without notice, she rips the paper down the middle, removing the mockingbird. Mulligan shows us how serious the use of hands are in the lives of the characters and how each one holds the power of life and death in his or her own hands. He conveys this message through close-up and long shots focusing on the hands. The use and expression of the hands in *To Kill a Mockingbird* symbolizes the power of life and death, the ability to create and destroy carried out by the central characters in the film.

Mulligan uses Jem's hand to initiate a connection between Jem, Scout and Boo Radley. The Radley house is the scariest house in the neighborhood and holds the most fascination for Jem, Scout and Dill. One afternoon, after rescuing Scout from a tire in the Radley yard, Jem, on a dare from Dill, touches the Radley's front door. This is a source of great pride and courage for Jem. However, it really is the first simple act of reaching out and making contact with Boo. This is the first event in the cause and effect chain, and Jem's hand symbolizes the bond of friendship being created between Jem, Scout and Boo. As Jem touches the door, Mulligan captures this action with a medium shot but keeps the hand centered in the frame.

One of the most powerful visual images in the film also occurs at the Radley house. Shortly after dark, on the same day that Jem touched the Radley door, the trio want to get a good look at Boo, so they sneak to the back of the house to look in a window. Jem is on the back porch with the other two nearby. Just when Jem is about to peak in the window, a very large, dark shadow of a man appears, cast on the side of the house, and begins moving towards Jem. Scout and Dill hide their eyes as the shadow of Boo Radley's hand passes slowly over Jem and is gone. In this scene the camera holds a tight close-up of Jem's back as the shadow of Boo's hand glides across it. The children react in fear; however, the opposite is the truth. The symbolic meaning is that Boo is watching over them, protecting them: "I have...covered you with the shadow of my hand" (Isaiah 51:16 [NIV]). From this powerful moment forward, the children realize that Boo will not hurt them.

Jem's hands are used to receive gifts of friendship from Boo. One day after school, as he is showing Scout how to walk like an Egyptian, they find two soap dolls that resemble Jem and Scout in the hollow of a tree in the corner of the Radley's front yard. Jem has found many other treasures in the tree prior to the soap dolls. Reminiscent of the opening scene, Mulligan again gives us a close-up look at the cigar box and its contents, this time with explanations, when later that night Jem shows Scout the treasures from the tree, a watch and chain, a pocket knife, a spelling medal, a locket, and various other items that he keeps in the cigar box. This is a very sweet and innocent use of friendly, receiving hands. They are appreciative of the little things because it is during the Depression, and they truly do not have much. The children's attitude has softened, even warmed, towards Boo, and they have become more accepting of him and less fearful than before, although they have not seen or met him.

In the trial scenes, hands and hand expressions are key. Mulligan shows how very destructive hands can be when they are used to destroy and not create and makes sure that we do not miss his point. In the scene when Mayella Ewell is sworn in and promises to tell the truth, the camera zooms in for a close-up as she places her right hand on the Bible. With this single act, she is sealing the fate of Tom Robinson. Mayella has no intention of telling the truth no matter what the consequences are for Tom. Hers, she feels, are greater. She would rather die than have the truth come out, and as she raises her hand and gives her testimony, in this point in history, no jury will decide against her. She even goes so far as to raise her right hand in the courtroom again to point Tom out as the man who raped her. Tom's innocent life is destroyed and ultimately lost by Mayella's ill use of her powerful hands.

Sharply contrasting the power in Mayella's hands, Mulligan shows the powerlessness in Tom Robinson's hands. Through the use of the long shot, Mulligan shows Tom taking his oath with the only good hand that he has, his right. Tom's left hand was injured when he was eight years old, and he is unable to move it. Atticus calls attention to this in a grand way as he makes an attempt to throw a glass to Tom and asks him to catch it with his left hand. Although he tells the whole, innocent truth, Tom is powerless to stop the jury's decision. Power is revealed through the hands. Tom is as powerless to sway the jury as he is to use his left hand.

Mulligan shows protective hands in two ways. In the scene in which Jem and Scout are walking home from their school's pageant, Scout is wearing her ham costume, so Jem is guiding her. Mulligan gives us a close-up of Jem's hand on the top of Scout's head as he grasps firmly, leading her in the proper direction. Their walk home is halted by Mr. Ewell's attack on Jem. During their struggle, the camera gives full attention to their hands. Jem frees himself to rush over to help Scout get up to run away; all the while the camera is keeping their hands in the frame. Mr. Ewell grabs Jem again, this time almost twisting his arm off, and pushes him to the ground. At this time Bob Ewell grabs Scout. The camera captures the struggle from Scout's low angle point of view but from a reverse shot position, keeping the hands in close-up range. The focus is around the small eye slit in Scout's ham costume as the struggle continues between two sets of hands fighting right in front of Scout's eyes. Scout watches as one set of hands takes the other set off of her and moves them away from her. The shadows of the hands, however, are cast on her, and we see one set of hands overpower the other set as the shadow of a hand remains on Scout. After the struggle is over, we see, through a long shot, Boo carrying Jem home with his powerfully protective hands.

In one of the sweetest scenes of the movie, Mulligan presents to us a close-up of nurturing hands as Scout reaches out to take the hand of Boo Radley to lead him out from behind the door. He has been behind the door ever since placing Jem in his bed, but, until now, no one has seen him there except Scout. She takes his hand gently and walks Boo over to Jem's bedside where she tells him that he can "pet" Jem. The camera finds Boo's hand and focuses on it as Boo hesitates to touch Jem. As Scout encourages him, the camera follows Boo's hand as it touches Jem's head. Then, as if Boo is remembering when the shadow of his hand passed over Jem the night on his back porch, he raises his hand so that its shadow once again covers Jem. Mulligan is very careful not to hurry this scene and keeps the focus on Boo's hand. Jem's arm is in a cast and lying on top of the bed; at this moment he is powerless. Scout takes Boo's hand in hers and leads him on to the front porch and to the swing where they sit together. Through the close-ups we can see that Scout's hands are nurturing towards Boo, while Boo's hands are accepting of hers and nurturing towards Jem.

Throughout the film, Mulligan shows Atticus's paternal hands wrapped around his children, especially Scout. Therefore, when Atticus picks up Scout and places her on the chair, he does so with all of the fatherly tenderness of a father who wants to hear what his daughter has to say. She has been elevated to his level when she says that to tell the town that Boo killed Mr. Ewell would be like "killing a mockingbird." As Scout is speaking, Atticus keeps his hands firmly placed on her shoulders. He only removes them to shake Boo's hand and to thank him for his children's lives. The camera captures this moment by keeping Atticus, Boo, and Scout in the frame with the shaking hands in the center of the frame. With this handshake, Atticus is agreeing to keep Boo's actions a secret, thus keeping him out of the limelight of the town women, thus giving him his life.

Mulligan ends the film with Scout walking Boo home hand in hand, leading him to his door, and waiting for him to go inside. Scout puts her hands in her pockets as if to save them and slowly walks past the Radley fence, then runs home. Mulligan zooms in through Jem's bedroom window to show Scout being held by Atticus's paternal hands as he watches over Jem. Mulligan shows the power of Atticus's hands through the power of his children's hands as they come to him for strength, for life.

Throughout the film, we are shown that the characters have the power of life and death, creation and destruction in their hands. We see the relationship between Jem and Scout bloom with Boo Radley, which all starts with a touch of Jem's hand on Boo's door. The fate of Tom Robinson is decided by Mayella's right hand on the Bible as she swears to tell the truth. We are shown the growth of two very eager young children in the loving, giving, paternal hands of their father, Atticus. Mulligan shows us that we all have the power of life and death in the palms of our hands, and it is up to us to decide how we will choose to use this power. We do not have to be in a sleepy southern town to know that the use and expression of our hands can symbolize the power of life and death in our own lives. We too can create and destroy, give and receive, nurture and be nurtured, protect and be protected, give life to or kill a mockingbird.

Satan: Dynamic in Flames and Static in Ice

By William Carrillo

English 2303: Literary Analysis, Comparison/Contrast

Satan is considered a universal symbol of all that is evil. Some think of him as a red devil with horns and a long tail. Others perceive him as a man with superhuman qualities. In literature, we find two conflicting depictions of him: Satan in Books 1 & 2 of Milton's *Paradise Lost*, and Lucifer in Canto 34 of Dante's *Inferno*. Contrasting the two is like contrasting a hero to a feeble slave, a captivating manipulator to a captive prisoner. Each is symbolically engulfed in his own element--Milton's in the ever-shifting flames of Hell, and Dante's in immobilizing ice. Yet both demonic figures are symbols of evil and punishment.

Milton initially presents Satan in *Paradise Lost* as a tragic hero who should be admired both for his physical stature as well as his superior leadership abilities. When we are first introduced to Satan, we are told of his "pride" that has caused him to be cast out of Heaven, along with his rebel angels. His "ambitious aim / Against the throne and monarchy of God" is with "vain attempt" (1.40-43). This, however, is not the end of Satan's "obdurate pride" (1.58), because his "will is unconquerable / He is filled with hate" (1.99-100). He has warred against God, the way that "Titanian [. . .] warred on Jove" (1.198).

Furthermore, his stature is comparable to his will, for Satan is huge in size with eyes

> That sparkling blazed; his other parts besides
> [. . .] extended long and large,
> [. . .] in bulk as huge
> As whom the fables name of monstrous size
> Briareous or Typhon [. . .]

> [. . .] or that sea-beast
> Leviathan, which God of all his works
> Created hugest that swim the ocean stream:
>   (1.194-202)

His enormous size is compared to the giants of mythology and the
Bible. Like the giants, Satan is a creation of God. Both he and the
giants rebel and fight against their creator(s). Satan was once
God's second-in-command, the "morning star," and is to be
admired for his former status in the realm of Heaven. Satan, as the
"fallen hero," carries his "ponderous shield / Ethereal temper,
massy, large, and round / [...] to equal which the tallest pine"
(1.284-5, 292). He uses his spear to aid him as he walks with
"uneasy steps" over the flames of Hell (1.295-296).

Yet Satan, even after his defeat in Heaven, cannot be
crushed so easily. He continues to command those who serve him
after their fall. In Hell's high capitol of Pandemonium, Satan sits
on his royal throne. He casts his eyes over Hell with its perpetual
flames. The fallen angels surround him and look upon him with
reverence. None other than Satan dares take the throne because no
one can endure the pain and suffering that Satan must. Here in this
kingdom of fallen angels, they gather for counsel to debate their
future. They look to Satan, for

> [. . .] none higher sat, with grave
> Aspéct he rose, and in his rising seemed
> A pillar of state, deep on his front engraven
> Deliberation sat and public care;
> And princely counsel in his face yet shone,
> Majestic though in ruin: sage he stood,
> With Atlantean shoulders fit to bear
> The weight of mightiest monarchies; his look
> Drew audience and attention still as night
> Or summer's noontime air, while thus he spake.
>   (2.300-309)

Satan offers them a new kingdom--Mankind's Eden. The new race
created by God will be less in power and excellence than those
whom Satan now rules. Through proper conniving and leadership,
the new creation may be destroyed. Better yet, Mankind could be
seduced to come to the fallen angels' side or, at least, be doomed

to Hell. Who in this group of rebel angels is so powerful, great, and cunning that he could endure this mission against God and His new race? Only one is truly heroic enough to face such a task. That one is "Satan, whom now transcendent glory raised / Above his fellows, with monarchal pride / Conscious of highest worth [. . .]" (2.427-429).

Satan is willing to champion the cause and move forward for the good of all those who have fallen. No "difficulty or danger, could deter" him (2.449). As ruler of his newly-established kingdom, he cannot refuse to accept the responsibility bestowed upon him by his legions. He courageously volunteers to leave and venture through the unknown and dangerous realm of Chaos in order to begin the corruption of mankind in the Garden of Eden, a frightening task which none of the other demons dares attempt.

Satan's willingness to be the hero of the fallen angels, to suffer and endure all that comes with reigning over this kingdom, is commendable. Because he is a leader of courageous stature and superior intelligence, it is no wonder why his angels "bend / With awful reverence prone; and as a god / Extol him equal to the Highest in Heaven" (2.477-479). This is Milton's Satan, a great giant, extreme in pride and enormous in size--prodigious and daring.

Lucifer in Dante's *Inferno* is almost the exact opposite. He is like an alien creature from another world, who possesses few recognizable human characteristics. Unlike Milton, Dante wants to present "the creature [Lucifer] that had once been so fair" (34.17-18), and "[i]f he were once [. . .] handsome [...] he is ugly now" (34.34). Although gigantic in size, his Lucifer is neither dynamic nor heroic. Rather, he is an imprisoned emperor of his "dolorous realm" (34.28). Lucifer presides at the bottom of a cavernous pit, created by his own fall from Heaven and over which he has little power. It is a realm which offers this "emperor" only the power to freeze his own tears into a glacial lake, entrapping sinners, often under the ice, in their stagnate, static rings, as he himself is held captive.

Dante's Lucifer cannot fly anywhere on his enormous bat-like wings because he is trapped, his "mid-breast protrud[ing] from ice" (34.29).   His three faces--one red, one black, and one yellowish-white--that sit upon his shoulders are fused at the top, a sad parody of the Holy Trinity:

The one in front [hatred] was fiery red;

the two others which were joined to it
over the middle of each shoulder
were fused together at the top.

The right one [impotence] seemed between white
and yellow;
the left [ignorance] was in color like those
who come from where the Nile rises. (34.38-44)

When looking at this beast, one experiences sadness and pity instead of awe because "[w]ith six eyes [he] wept and over his three chins / He let tears drip and bloody foam" (34.53-54).   His back is stripped of skin due to constant scratching, and his bat-like wings beat with a futile force, for the only effect is to freeze the Cocytus River into a solid sheet of ice.   His hair is frozen, tangled tufts.   This Lucifer is no beautiful hero to be worshipped, but an ice-entrapped, pitiful giant.

The only souls Lucifer has the power to punish are the three upon whom he chews.   Looking at Lucifer's red face and peering into that mouth, one can see Judas Iscariot. "His head is inside the mouth, and he kicks with his legs" (34.62-63).   In the black mouth is Brutus who "twists and says nothing" (34.65).   In the yellow-white mouth is Cassius who "seems so heavy" (34.67). Lucifer chews on them, like someone chewing a tobacco leaf, chomping down with no thought of action, just never-ending mastication.   Instead of being cunning and powerful like Milton's Satan, Dante's Lucifer is represented as stupid and impotent.   He is, in fact, so impotent that Dante and Virgil are able to cross over him and climb out of Hell by clutching his frozen tufts.   Lucifer does not even twitch.

The elements that link both versions of Satan are hate and evil incarnate. Milton gives Satan an expansive realm over which to rule, as well as the possibility of capturing Eden, the Earthly Paradise. Satan in *Paradise Lost* commands respect for the destruction he can and will cause. *Inferno's* Lucifer cannot exercise his powers because he is frozen in the depths of the Earth. God condemns him to the lowest region of a frozen Hell with other sinners cast there. Milton, on the other hand, a believer in the doctrine of free will, gives Satan freedom to reign over the evil angels and ultimately corrupt Mankind by tempting Adam and Eve to disobey God. Dante's Lucifer does not even govern Hell itself. He and the ice freeze together into a single sheet of near-paralysis. Milton's Prince of Darkness, like the dark flames themselves, is lively, fluid, and dynamic. He is in apparent control of his realm and is its fiery center of activity.

Whether dynamic in action or statically frozen in Hell, Satan and Lucifer represent all that should be avoided by humankind, as well as the punishment that will result if evil is not avoided. Because the Satans of Milton and Dante contrast starkly, each author affects his readers in a different way. Although each author seeks to present a being that is to be feared or shunned because of the evil he represents, it is up to the reader to determine which description of absolute evil is the one that corresponds more to his or her beliefs. In either case, the reader will be compelled to consider that the Monarch of Hell was once God's most powerful angel, a further reason for taking the threat of his authority seriously.

Works Cited

Dante. "The Inferno." Trans. H. R. Huse. <u>Literature of the Western World</u>. Ed. Brian Wilkie and James Hurt. 4th ed. Vol. 1. Upper Saddle River, New Jersey: Prentice Hall, 1997. 1384-1522. 2 vols.

Milton, John. "Paradise Lost." <u>Literature of the Western World</u>. Ed. Brian Wilkie and James Hurt. 4th ed. Vol. 1. Upper Saddle River, New Jersey: Prentice Hall, 1997. 2111-2208. 2 vols.

The Steep Side of Humility

By Angie Mabry

English 2312: Literary Analysis, Comparison/Contrast

One of the most powerful messages was given from a mountain; Christ's Sermon on the Mount not only set the standards for those who would follow Him, it appears God Himself confirmed that hills do indeed make the best podiums. In the literal sense, James Baldwin's *Go Tell it On the Mountain* concurs with the basic idea that when one's deepest convictions lead one to proclaim them from the highest places, positions of both power and visibility, clearly one's message should ring with certainty. Baldwin's story centers around a "telling of the ultimate" from those places on high, and it is obvious his main character's passion and convictions lead him up there, but he is unable to deliver once he gets there; it is impossible for him to share that which he cannot fully comprehend--namely, the grace and mercy of a forgiving Father who gives welcome to the weak and hope to the forlorn. The message itself appears to be what Baldwin is most interested in getting across to the reader. Through the character of Gabriel Grimes, he presents an example of the message gone awry, of the messenger who, in his urgency and fear, has forgotten to take the message. In many ways, Baldwin's classic story of the troubled father and son relationship greatly resembles the relationship between father and son in Jesus' parable of the Prodigal Son.

Gabriel and the unnamed Prodigal share similar family backgrounds; both come from a "wealth" of sorts; one experiences it in the monetary sense while the other in terms of faith. The young men share a penchant for self destruction, each going off into symbolic "far-away lands" to satisfy the desires of their hearts. Finally and most importantly, the character contrast sets up an interesting parallel regarding the "return to the Father." The Prodigal is reluctant to go home to his father because he knows he has squandered his wealth through reckless living. He then doubts his position within the household, assuming his actions have made him totally unacceptable to his father, while Gabriel's return from his own wild lifestyle through salvation is marred by self-doubt, a belief about himself which projects itself onto his relationship with his step-son John.

Wealth is interpreted in a variety of ways; while the Prodigal's is described in Luke 15:12 as being in terms of "his share of his father's estate," Gabriel's wealth is conveyed in a spiritual sense and comes in the form of a praying mother. In terms of religious tradition, one is considered wealthy when one comes from a home rich in the "heritage of faith." It is often from these homes that great spiritual leaders emerge, i.e. the Grahams, the Schullers. Gabriel was not lacking in this respect. His mother's prayers were vigilant; on her deathbed she "prayed for him, sitting up in her bed unaided, her head lifted, her voice steady; while he, kneeling in a corner of the room, trembled and almost wished that she would die" (Baldwin 93). Similarly, the Prodigal's father was vigilant in his watchfulness for his son; "while he was still a long way off, he [father] saw him and was filled with compassion, running to him and throwing his arms around his [son's] neck" (Luke 15:20). To see the son from a long way off meant he must have been waiting and watching for his return, much like Gabriel's mother and her refusal to die, "lingering only for his surrender to the Lord" (Baldwin 93). Both the Prodigal and Gabriel share the gift of godly parents, a gift which has not been fully appreciated until recently in modern society. Ironically, the wisdom concerning such principles has endured for centuries, lying quietly and unobtrusively within the diary pages of the Father of Time Himself.

In the spirit of the old cliche "boys will be boys," both unwittingly trade self-control and discernment for a little excitement and the opportunity to tell dear old dad he was wrong. Setting off for the distant twinkle of far-away lands, they leave behind the security of home and faith in search of a "soul hole"

151

filler. Believing they will find something they lack, one goes many miles across the country; the other goes to countless bars and cat-houses away from the mother who seemingly gives death a no thank-you, while she awaits the promise of the Lord for her son. In a spiritual realm, the parallel of the far country for both characters is the same: a separation from the truth.

Both Gabriel and the Prodigal eventually find that these things of the world do not satisfy the longing of the soul. Coming to these painful conclusions, Gabriel is faced with his total inability to manage his life; "he hated the evil that lived in his body, and he feared it, as he feared and hated the lions of lust and longing that prowled the defenseless city of his mind" (Baldwin 94). The far-off lands of pleasure lead both to physical and spiritual poverty, as both discover; the Prodigal, "finding himself in need after a severe famine in that land," is reduced to feeding pigs, "longing to fill his stomach with the pods that the pigs were eating" (Luke 15:16), while Gabriel's spiritual condition places him "in mud, in strange beds, and once or twice in jail; his mouth sour, his clothes in rags, from all of him arising the stink of his corruption" (Baldwin 94). Though the degrees are different in all people, the spiritual results are the same; the soul's condition without the light of Truth is one of darkness and confusion. Baldwin illustrates this point using the extremes; Gabriel must come to the bottom of his fleshly addictions to realize his dependency on God.

The return of both the Prodigal and Gabriel to the Father, one earthly, the other Heavenly, sets up striking similarities in that both have an intense fear of being turned away by the father. Both seem convinced their actions warrant total separation from the identities into which they were born. The Prodigal believes "he has sinned against heaven and against his father and that he is no longer worthy to be called his son" (Luke 15:21), while Gabriel's guilt over past actions distorts his view of who his Father is and of the reality of the gift of grace he has been given. Throughout his entire life, Gabriel's fear of punishment, his fear of losing his salvation causes him to doubt his true identity, his true identity as a precious child of the King, wholly lovable and forgiven:

Then, trembling, he got out of bed again and washed himself. It was a warning and he knew it, and he seemed to see before him the pit dug by Satan--deep and silent, waiting for him. He thought of the dog returned to his vomit, of the man who had been cleansed, and who fell, and who was possessed by seven devils, the last state of that man being worse than the first. (Baldwin 111).

This fear separates him from the Father who forgives and forgets, and causes him to approach Him much like the Prodigal approaches his own father saying, "I am no longer worthy to be called your son; make me like one of your hired men" (Luke 15:19). Here the Prodigal, like Gabriel, is saying to his father, "I am not worthy of your love. I will continue to live in filthy rags of guilt and shame; I will continue to approach you as a step-son, a hired hand; I will live as one cut off from the family." It is out of this guilt and shame that Gabriel turns his self-loathing toward his wife, Elizabeth, and his step-son, John, making them pay, as his sister Florence points out, for his own sins: "I know you thinking at the bottom of your heart that if you just make her, her and her bastard boy, pay enough for her sin, your son won't have to pay for yours [. . . .] it's time you started paying" (Baldwin 214).

The theme of payment for sins is strong throughout the novel, as it is with the parable of the Prodigal Son. it is a recurring message which seems to haunt and imprison all its characters. It is a message void of grace and mercy; it is one which seems to have gone awry during the journey, during the times in the far-off lands both "sons" have experienced. The separation has blinded them to the truth; the payment both long to give to the Father has already been paid.

Works Cited

Baldwin, James. Go Tell it On the Mountain. New York: Dell, 1952.

Holy Bible. New International Version. Grand Rapids: Zondervan, 1986.

PRELIMINARY OR WORKING OUTLINE
The Steep Side of Humility

<u>Thesis</u>: In many ways, Baldwin's classic story of a father and son's troubled relationship greatly resembles the relationship between father and son in Jesus' parable of the Prodigal Son.

1. Both grow up in families surrounded by wealth and love.
    a. Prodigal--monetary wealth
    b. Gabriel--"heritage of belief" wealth
    c. Both young men had parents who were vigilant in their waiting/praying for them.

2. Both share a penchant for self-destruction (both went to far-off lands).
    a. Prodigal--a physical far-off land
    b. Gabriel--an emotional far-off land
    c. Both young men found that wine, women, and song did not fill them spiritually.

3. Both experienced a sense of fear and dread when approaching "the Father."
    a. Prodigal--was satisfied to work as a hired hand for his father.
    b. Gabriel--was satisfied to suffer in his guilt and shame, not embracing his Father's love and complete acceptance.
    c. Both young men did not fully understand a Father's love for his children.

Anne Rivers Siddons' novel *Peachtree Road* explores the social structure of the affluent community of Buckhead from 1940 until the 1980's—the most tumultuous time in Atlanta's recent history. By interweaving the tragic characters of Lucy Bondurant and Ben Cameron, Jr., both Buckhead citizens, with Atlanta's Negro community and the growing homosexual community, respectively, Siddons allows us to see the devastating consequences of prejudice. Strong opposition to diversity by the conservative inhabitants of Buckhead contributes directly to the suicides of both Lucy and Ben. The inflexible attitudes encountered in their everyday environments give them no viable means of emotional support for each of their complex and unique personalities. Buckhead, their home, failed them.

The very first line of *Peachtree Road* begins with, "The South killed Lucy [. . .]" (Siddons 3). While this is a correct observation, a more precise statement is, "Buckhead killed Lucy." It is hard to say whether Lucy would have survived if she had grown up in her hometown of New Orleans, but she would have had a better chance. Lucy's personality, like the city of New Orleans, is exciting, loose, and chaotic; Atlanta, and especially Buckhead, with its rigid, time-honored rules, can never change Lucy, or accept her as she is, and, even as a child, "Lucy did not like to be contradicted" (14).

Buckhead is a money town (6). Money, and the appearance of money, is of the utmost importance to the elite families of Buckhead. Lucy's straightforward attitude is a tremendous obstacle to her fitting into her new home. We get our first glimpse of this problem at Sarah's sixth birthday party, when Lucy criticizes the entertainment (55). If not for Ben Cameron's sensitive intervention, Lucy's induction into Buckhead's young society might have been a disaster.

Lucy is not without her positive qualities. For a time, Lucy's fearlessness makes her a champion among the young boys of Buckhead. She leads the bicycle forays throughout Buckhead, and beyond. Unfortunately, her daring personality, even among the boys, eventually proves to be too much. The demolition of the Pink Castle, which she instigates, and the subsequent discovery by the Buckhead police, is more than the young boys can tolerate (116). The strict moral code taught to the boys of Buckhead appears, at times, to be born in them. They all have limits--limits Lucy can never accept. That incident ends the camaraderie, and more importantly, the power Lucy has held over the boys. This illustrates very clearly how her inability to conform leaves her miserably lonely, despite periods of popularity (118). It also explains her intense attraction to the Negroes and their causes of the times.

Because of Lucy's strong feelings of loss after her father's desertion, she is constantly searching for acceptance and love. This is first seen in her demands of Shep as a young boy (44). Therefore, when, at a very young age, the Negro housekeeper, Martha Cater, takes care of Lucy after she is isolated from the rest of the family as punishment, Lucy develops a strong affection for the black woman and her family. Lucy feels as though they understand and love her for who she is, with no conditions (313). Because Lucy meets Negroes who are considered "middle class," she and her new friends are able to develop mutual, trusting friendships--friendships that are vitally important to Lucy.

Lucy's feverish crusade for black equality, in part fueled by her mental illness, becomes the final blow to the community of Buckhead. With all its rules of society, Buckhead has no room for Lucy and her growing eccentricities. Even though some residents of Buckhead are sympathetic toward the Negroes' plight, Lucy's own family is "totally united in their disapproval of Lucy's association with 'that crazy radical [Martin Luther King, Jr.] and the niggers down there'" (314). Lucy, abandoned again, clings even more tightly to her own dreams and her own world. Her zealous fight for civil rights for the Negroes intensifies at a rate equal to her mental illness, illustrated when Martin Luther King, Jr. is assassinated, and Lucy suffers the first of her major mental breakdowns (433).

Lucy's best hope for sanity comes in a man named Jack Venable (314). He, too, works for the Civil Rights' Movement, so they share a common goal. Lucy needs a calm, rational person in her life who will accept her as she is, and Jack is all that. The only problem is that Jack comes along too late. Lucy, already addicted to tension, turmoil, and the "glamour" of the movement, cannot stop herself from spiraling out of control (441). Her suicide is inevitable.

Even though Shep uses her mental illness to encourage her to shoot herself, she is already on a path to total annihilation (562). The murder of her husband shows unmistakably Lucy's total loss of her mind. If her family, and the entire community of Buckhead, did not place so many restrictions on her--all because of appearances--she might have found a more productive way of living her damaged life. Perhaps, if she felt accepted, she would not be so compelled to shock the people around her. Unfortunately, most of the adults try to distance themselves from Lucy. Besides Shep, the Cameron adults are probably the only Buckhead residents who naturally sense Lucy's vulnerability, but they do nothing to help her, and, regrettably, while their sights are aimed at Lucy for a time, they are oblivious to their own son's impending crisis.

Ben, like Lucy, is different from his Buckhead peers. He is just much better at hiding it with his heterosexual marriage. Hindsight reveals Ben's knowledge of his dilemma on his wedding day, when Shep notices how uncomfortable Ben is at his wedding to Julia Randolph (270). Ben already knows his homosexuality, like Lucy's affection for the Negroes, will never be accepted in his strict community, so he begins the first of many deceptions to preserve his reputation, both for himself and for his family.

Another indication of Ben's growing anxiety over his terrible secret is the conversation between him and Shep on the eve of the stroke of Shep's father (355). When Ben says that he has the "mark of Cain," he is referencing his homosexuality and the knowledge he has of the ramifications he will face if anyone ever finds him out (356). He specifically acknowledges the choking hold the people of Buckhead have on his life (356). Ben's displeasure with his heterosexual living arrangement is also made evident by his "meanspirited" comment about pregnant women while his own wife is pregnant (357). This is the first real warning of his impending demise.

As with Lucy, Shep is not the only Buckhead resident to notice Ben's unhappiness. Ben's family is aware of the change in his personality, but, living in the sheltered community of Buckhead, they cannot imagine anything troublesome enough to warrant suicide (460). The revelation that Julia knows of his homosexuality and uses it to blackmail him into submission to her illustrates the severe punishment Ben will suffer from all of Buckhead, should they know of his sexual affinity (457).

After Ben's death and the subsequent disclosure of his homosexuality to his family, the fact that the family can never tell anyone the true cause of Ben's suicide is the strongest case against Buckhead for its role in this tragedy (459). Sarah's acknowledgement of the lack of support for her brother in his time of need also becomes an admission of weakness of character (460). Her desire for continued acceptance in society overshadows her concern for Ben. Buckhead does not teach its young how to "ward off demons and monstrousness and loss" (460). They only learn how to enjoy a "normal" life.

The residents of Buckhead are fundamentally good people. They are just narrow-minded when it comes to one of their own. The Negroes' fight for equal rights is acknowledged, and sympathy is extended to them for their struggle, but, except for Lucy, and, in a less obvious way, the elder Ben Cameron, no one joins in their fight. Homosexuality, also somewhat tolerated in outsiders, is completely unthinkable within their own boundaries. Distance from adversity and diversity makes the Buckhead populace feel safe in their cocoon of wealth and status.

Since Ben and Lucy are obviously unable to fit into the molds that Buckhead has for each of them upon their arrival there-- Ben by birth, Lucy by fate--they have to make their own paths in order to find the world in which they belong. Lucy, with her mental illness, is probably not able to comprehend the grave errors she makes in her life, according to Buckhead standards. The very love she seeks is available there, but she does not know how to secure it. Possibly, given her vibrant personality, she may not have remained within the confines of Buckhead, anyway. However, if the community had not ostracized her, she might have sought help from someone within it--people with the knowledge and the extraordinary means to assist someone suffering as Lucy does.

Ben, on the other hand, is well aware of his predicament. "Atlanta is a murderously bad city for a homosexual [. . .]" during Ben's lifetime. (459). Ben himself has participated in harassing and degrading obvious homosexuals in his early days (459). There is not enough time in Ben's life for him to wait for acceptance. He is desperately in love with a man, and the only way he can escape the agony of his double life is through death. Atlanta, especially Buckhead, has shown him that, with exposure, his life will be over anyway. His career would be destroyed; his reputation, and possibly his family's reputation, would be stained forever by his terrible sin. Scandal and ostracism would follow him the rest of his life. He cannot bring that burden on the family and friends he loves.

Buckhead, for all its wealth and status, is not a good place for someone like either Ben or Lucy to grow up. Strict moral codes are unable to bend enough to allow any uniqueness to enter its righteous circle. Turning their backs on their loved ones is preferred to conceding to the perceived lower standards of the middle-class, from which they constantly detach themselves--even

159

if it means death for a daughter and a son, a sister and a brother, a mother and a father--two people who have a great deal to offer, not just to Buckhead, but also to the entire world.

Work Cited

Siddons, Anne Rivers. <u>Peachtree Road</u> New York: Harper and
    Row, 1988.

Whitman's Waltz: Dancing Outside the Box (A Literary Discussion of "Song of Myself")
By Tracy Kirkpatrick
English 2310: Literary Analysis, Researched

As the longest and most famous (or infamous) piece within Walt Whitman's *Leaves of Grass*, "Song of Myself" continues to resonate in the ears of those who listen intently, even close to 150 years after its original publication. (Whitman went on to republish *Leaves of Grass* numerous times until his death at the end of the 19th century.) When he first presented it in 1855, Whitman shocked readers with his petite edition of *Leaves of Grass*--to the point that he lost his job at the Department of the Interior on the grounds of immorality--and today, readers still labor and deliberate over Whitman's intent, vernacular, and underlying messages. Whatever the reader's view might be on Whitman and his unparalleled verse in "Song of Myself," one cannot deny Russell Blakenship's observation that "it [*Leaves of Grass*] was original; nothing quite like it had previously appeared in the world of literature" (348).

While some critics have been quick to dismiss "Song of Myself" as an egotistical outpouring of Whitman's non-conformist views, it is irrefutable that he is indeed a breaker of boundaries both thematically and stylistically in this forthright piece of literature. Employing writing styles not readily used in the world of poetry and themes not yet touched upon (or at least to his vivid extreme), Whitman not only crosses the line of traditional literary genres, he removes the ties that constrain us as readers. Through his underlying message of equality--between human and nature, between the writer and the reader--we clearly realize that not only is this poem a melody for Whitman, it is a harmonious tune for the entire world. Whitman records in the 1855 "Preface" in *Leaves of Grass*, "The messages of great poets to each man and woman are, Come to us on equal terms, Only then can you understand us, We are no better than you, What we enclose you enclose, What we enjoy you may enjoy" (2735).

This unmistakable yet indiscernible idea, that poets and the common person could be equal, severed the fiber that had dominated, although at times unspoken, early literary writings: manifestation of the religious and political causes espoused by Whitman's predecessors. As can been seen in the writings of the pre-colonial times up though the first part of the 1800's, literary expressions were limited to the identification and behavior of Americans, conveyed in the manner of an address or lecture and based upon the fear of the future or relation of the past. Whitman's certainty that poetry must reach the reader on his or her own accord allowed him "to contradict predecessors, to challenge convention [. . .]" (Vance 129).

To provide the background of American Literature preceding the era of Walt Whitman would be equal in length to many research papers. However, to appreciate the way in which the writings of Whitman, specifically "Song of Myself," oppose his literary forerunners and disrupt the line of traditional American myths, we must first have a basic understanding of what came prior to Whitman's time. Early in the 16th century, following the evolution of oral tradition to written passage, the earliest colony settlers began to write of exploration and new world experiences, expressed in old world language. These authors wrote with passion and fervor in their descriptions, recounting their journeys, discoveries and hopes. Though these journals offer current-day readers an insight into the struggles of this period in America, the true goal of pre-colonial explorers was to relate the findings and benefits of this recently "discovered" land back to the financiers of their voyages.

As the diverse population of the colonies continued to grow over time, so too did the variations on religious beliefs. People of all sects were privy to the written doctrines of their religion, based in part upon the creed of the church, and mostly upon the writers' interpretations of the message-du-jour. Literary ambassadors such as Jonathan Edwards, a leader of the Great Awakening revival,

164

alerted his congregation with a horrendous urgency that, "all you that were never born again, [. . .] are in the hands of an angry God" (598), likening the Lord's actions to those of an unjust, unmerciful serial killer. Subsequent religious writings of the mid 1700's present a more loving image of God, as seen in John Woolman's *Journal of John Woolman*. From Woolman and his shared beliefs with the Society of Friends (Quakers), we learn about the simplicity of life, the equality of all God's creatures, and the universal rule of tenderness, which all mankind should abide.

With the Enlightenment era and the rise of empirical sciences, American literature gleaned the graces of extraordinary thinkers and significant authors such as Benjamin Franklin, John Locke and Thomas Jefferson. Notwithstanding the various themes of the early American writers (exploration, religion and politics), all had this in common: the formation and identity of America. Whitman was not quick to abandon these American themes in his writing; nevertheless, the style and language of his writing ruptured the seams of mainstream publication ideals. As a reader, one witnesses the reflections of the perils of 19th century democracy (labor, women's rights, slavery, and the state of the nation as a whole). Standing apart from comparative literary works, however, "Song of Myself" invokes a use of "I" that forever changed the face of American literature. "Whitman's act of self naming represented an assault on literary decorum and [. . .] the New England literary establishment" (Erkkila 2725).

William Vance further expands this examination of the proverbial "you" when he says, "Ambiguous in number, gender and relation, the 'you' has largely replaced an obsession, over the last several decades, with the nature of the 'Self' that speaks in the poems" (132). With the exception of literary champions such as Emerson and Thoreau, Whitman's non-confinement within the boundaries of 19th century poetry thrust him to the forefront of a new literary movement, which would later affect great writers such as Emily Dickinson and Carl Sandburg. As attentive readers of Whitman, we must believe that his definition of a great poet and his effort to fulfill that vision is what ultimately shattered preconceived concepts of American poetry. For even in the

"Preface" to *Leaves of Grass*, Whitman says of the greatest poet, "he places himself where the future becomes the present" (2734).

"Whitman's radically original style is characterized by an expansive demotic vocabulary, rhythmically balanced long lines that are complete units, and above all a reconception [sic] of the reader's role" (Vance 132-33). Creating verse that extends beyond the limitations of time necessitates an understanding of and sympathy with the common person. Beyond that, the writer must have the ability to communicate with, rather than speak to, the reader. Unlike his predecessors, Whitman made demands of his poetry, not of its readers. While Whitman was not the originator of the English language, the way in which he twisted its use transcended even that of his literary peers. Callow and Reilly summarize Whitman's inventive delivery by saying, "Whitman believed that poems should unfold naturally; he disliked ornamentation, and he insisted that thought always came first within him, sound second" (161). Whitman's unique exercise of words places himself and all people at the same level, as seen with the natural language and straightforward style of "Song of Myself":

> Walt Whitman, an American, one of the roughs, a kosmos,
> Disorderly fleshy and sensual. . . . eating drinking and breeding,
> No sentimentalist. . . . no stander above men and women or apart from them . . . . no more modest than immodest. (24.499-501)

More than the refusal of allowing elaborate words to stand in the way of his message, the manner in which Whitman delivers prose opens up the reader's receptiveness to his message. Although writers prior to Whitman such as Woolman and Jefferson, without debate, believed in equality in some form or fashion, Whitman turns the pages of American literature by relating every one to a fundamental common denominator, that which can be broken down no further: "I celebrate myself, / And what I assume you shall assume, / For every atom belonging to me as good belongs to you" ("Song" 1.1-3). Throughout "Song of Myself," Whitman

166

bends the conventional principles of American poetry by reaffirming his sense that we are equivalent: "In all people I see myself, none more and not one a barleycorn less, / And the good or bad I say of myself I say of them" (20.401-02). Tossing aside the conventions of time-honored poets and collapsing the traditions of acceptable language and style, word-by-word Whitman consciously crafted his verse.

A reader of "Song of Myself" does not need to be an expert on Whitman, comprehend the meaning or significance of his verse or be a poet to realize the obvious: the poem does not rhyme. He uses no formal meter and seems to let the words run randomly across, nearly off, the page. This style of Whitman's can be likened to that of an artist who paints an abstract painting. To the uneducated eye, it is nothing more than globs of paint, deceptively without meaning. However, one must remember that an abstract painting is not the sign of a poor artist. After all, no one observing Picasso's abstract *Dora Maar* (France 1939) could dare utter the words that he is not a skillful, talented artist. Similarly, one cannot reject Whitman's capability to prudently create his verse simply because it does not represent what people commonly think of as poetry. Take, for example, these lines from "Song of Myself":

Where the panther walks to and fro on a limb overhead ....
    where the buck turns furiously at the hunter,
Where the rattlesnake suns his flabby length on a rock ....
    where the otter is feeding on the fish,
Where the alligator in his tough pimples sleeps by the bayou,
Where the black bear is searching for roots or honey ....
    where the beaver pats the mud with his paddle-tail;
    [..]
Where the katydid works her chromatic reed on the walnut-tree over the well;   (33.720-23, 769)

At first glance, one may think that Whitman has disrespectfully thrown the words upon the page. However, readers of early literature know that this technique of repetition is not altogether brand new. Most often, the reiteration found within verse is of that found in Native American chants.

167

In looking at the Zuni's *Sayatasha's Night Chant*, we learn that this particular recurrence of words and images represents the materialization of a plentiful future:

> That you may grow old,
> That you may have corn,
> That you may have beans,
> That you may have squash,
> That you may have wheat,
> That you may kill game,
> That you may be blessed with riches,
> For all this I asked. (166-173)

Algis Valiunas remarks on Whitman's unusual poetry tactics, saying that his desire to fill his poetry with as much life as possible led to the requirement of "a poetic form more elastic and accommodating than traditional verse" (71). The elongated, undulating lines of Whitman's verse carry a melodic sound, and not unlike the mantra of *Sayatasha's Night Chant*, one can imagine vocalizing the lyrics of Whitman's free verse, most properly entitled "<u>Song</u> of Myself" [emphasis added]:

> The smoke of my own breath,
> Echos, ripples, and buzzed whispers. . . . loveroot,
> silkthread , crotch and vine,
> My respiration and inspiration. . . . the beating of
> my heart. . . . . (2.13-15)

"Whitman himself likened his verse to the irregular breaking of waves on the shore" (Callow and Reilly 162), which is the most fitting way to describe the irregular and at times irrational splintering of Whitman's rebellious verse. Whitman wrote unconventionally, neglecting rhyme and reason, but all the while cognizant of his intent: to converse with the reader.

Methods other than the musical rhythm of verse come into play when discussing the lines of "Song of Myself," namely Whitman's ability to capture the reader. Not only do Whitman's eloquent words entice us to the door, he invites us into his house, luring us with secrets by saying, "These things I tell you in confidence, / I might not tell everybody but I will tell you" (19.386-87). According to Gayle Smith, "[R]eaders and critics have sought to resolve the interviewed [sic] issues of style,

intention and relationship to the reader in Whitman's poetry"
(151). "Song of Myself" takes the notion of equality one step
further by speaking so intimately with his readers, that he collapses
the framework we recognize as long-established poetry:

> Stop this day and night with me and you shall possess
> the origin of all poems,
> You shall possess the good of the earth and sun. . . .
> there are millions of suns left,
> You shall no longer take things at second or third hand
> …. nor look through the eyes of the dead …. nor
> feed on the spectres in books,
> You shall not look through my eyes either, nor take
> things from me,
> You shall listen to all sides and filter them from
> yourself. (2.25-29)

The words expressed by Whitman not only imply a dialogue
between poet and reader, they serve as a means of encouragement
to access the inner ability of universal understanding that each of
us has, a belief that most likely stems from Whitman's
transcendentalist views.

Popular in America during the 1840's, transcendentalism is
neither a religion nor a philosophy, but rather a concern for daily
living. With a faith in humankind, an affinity for nature, a
consciousness of the present, and an identification of oneself with
the universe, transcendentalist influences of former writers are
obvious in Whitman's writing. Those with a minimum of literary
knowledge are aware of Emerson's influence on Whitman,
regarding which Russell Blakenship comments, "The startling
ideas of transcendentalism were so expressed [. . .] that they
seemed wholly original and far more startling than those of
Emerson" (348); he then further states, "In a record of Whitman's
conversations covering only a little more than a year, Emerson is
mentioned about two hundred times" (353). While the literary
world is certainly aware that Whitman did not coin ideas of
transcendentalism and was not the first writer to have these ideals
as an underlying theme, Whitman's style, verse and imagery push
the threshold to its upper most limit.

169

Though the effects of Whitman's transcendentalist views can be been seen in "Song of Myself," they should not be taken as the main theme of the literature. Regarding Whitman's beliefs in relation to humankind and nature as portrayed in his work, Russell Blankenship writes, "It is true that Whitman, as a transcendentalist of the Emerson school, was far from despising nature, but his great love was all mankind, with whom he felt an utter identity" (71). When looking at "Song of Myself," we see an ever-hopeful Whitman avow, again with his distinctive style of personalization:

> Failing to fetch me at first keep encouraged,
> Missing me one place search another,
> I stop some where waiting for you   (52.1334-36)

Even without a vast number of references to nature, Whitman establishes early within "Song of Myself" that the purity of the environment and openness to nature are important:

> The atmosphere is not a perfume …. it has no taste
>   of the distillation …. it is odorless,
> It is in my mouth forever …. I am in love with it,
> I will go to the bank by the wood and become
>   undisguised and naked,
> I am mad for it to be in contact with me. (2.9-12)

Also important to the transcendentalist belief is the precept of time, in that time is the only thing that constrains us from doing that which is pleasing. Whitman explains the importance of treating each moment with equal respect when he says, "This minute that comes to me over the past decillions [sic], / There is no better than it and now" ("Song" 22.479-80). Aside from the commonality of optimism, nature and present-day, Whitman's transcendental themes were mild in comparison to other writers of his day, and it was not these aspects that made "Song of Myself" famous. Once more, Russell Blakenship notes about Whitman, "He considered it [human nature] divine, and he went one step beyond the New Englanders in insisting that the body, the home of the soul, is equally divine with the spirit" (357). Incontrovertibly, the organic language in "Song of Myself" reveals a message not hidden: "I have said that the soul is not more than the body, / And I have said that the body is not more than the soul [. . .]" (48.1262-63). Still, as radical as Whitman's views, language and style may

170

have been for their time, they did not contribute to the notoriety of "Song of Myself" as did his explosive sexual imagery.

Most infamous and widely skimmed over of Whitman's "Song of Myself" is section three containing verse about Whitman's rendezvous with God: "As God comes a loving bedfellow and sleeps at my side all night and close on the peep of the day" [. . .] (3.52). Astonishing 19th and 21st century readers alike, Whitman's merging of the sexes and vivid sexual imagery catapulted him into a realm of literature unknown. Gene Bluestein says of Whitman's methods that he is "a pioneer in the development of poetic techniques, so was he the forerunner of contemporary sexual ideas and attitudes" (154). Lavish sexual entendres do not fail to elude the reader of "Song of Myself" with language to describe "[w]inds whose soft-tickling genitals rub against me [. . .]" (24.542). The lines of sexual identity are broken when Whitman proclaims, "I am the poet of the woman the same as the man, / And I say it is as great to be a woman as to be a man [. . .]" (21.426-27). Whitman represents no shame in his sexual images and at times goes to great length to expand the horizons of American literature, especially in section five:

> Loafe with me on the grass …. loose the stop from your
> throat,
>
> Not words, nor music or rhyme I want …. not custom
> or lecture, not even the best,
> Only the lull I like, the hum of your valved voice.
>
> I mind how we lay in June, such a transparent summer
> morning;
> You settled your head athwart my hips and gently
> turned over upon me,
> And parted the shirt from your bosom-bone, and
> plunged your tongue to my barestript heart,
> And reached till you felt my beard, and reached until
> you held my feet. (5.75-81)

In speaking of Whitman's bold poetry, William Vance remarks that Whitman has undertaken a "breaking of cultural bonds restricting knowledge of the body, its functions and its pressures, and so breaking also the bonds of sexual repression and secrecy, gender definition, and sexual identity" (161). The impish writing and sexual imagery used throughout "Song of Myself" remind readers of a primal instinct that transcends our basic, universal understanding of birth, death and love. Ways in which Whitman bends the meaning of the language invoke in each of us a sense of passion that reaches far beyond the pages of a book.

Whether one is a literary buff or novice of poetry, the verse of Walt Whitman is sure to remain forever engraved upon the minds of his readers. Both stylistically and thematically, "Song of Myself" continues to erase the conventional rules of poetry, even literature in its entirety, with its bold language, expression of ideas, and vivid, "makes you blush" sexual imagery. Whitman's use of words not only transforms the English language, it places the reader in a dimension where human, spirit and earth elude the boundaries of each other and time.

"Days of yore" writers brought with them religious dogma, political agendas, and the identity of America in the face of exploration, toil and growth. It was not until Whitman that the world of literature, and the world at large, became exposed to his shocking style of expression, intertwining faith in human nature with the inner sense of spirit and our relationship as people to both the physical and supernatural worlds. Although "Song of Myself" certainly does not introduce any radical beliefs or extremist ideals in the overall concept of American literature, the way in which Whitman presents his thoughts shocked his contemporaries in the mid-19th century and still makes some turn their heads away in embarrassment today.

Whitman's desire to obtain the status of a time-honored poet undoubtedly became fulfilled with the publishing of "Song of Myself," his verse breaking down boundaries and forging new ground on the frontier of American literature.

In researching Walt Whitman, one can find diverse opinions on his personality, lifestyle and work. Admirers of Whitman hail him as a brilliant, ageless literary hero, while critics are quick to judge him as a talented egotist. If, as Whitman suggests, each of us is made up of man, woman, nature and spirit, then it is safe to assume what Whitman assumes: "I am large. . . .I contain multitudes" ("Song" 51.1316). Realizing Whitman's robustness, readers can only continue to speculate on the vast meaning of "Song of Myself" and come to their own conclusions based upon their knowledge, experience and understanding. Or, maybe we should just enjoy Whitman's work for what it is, keeping in mind the words of another great poet, Carl Sandburg, "I have written some poetry that I don't understand myself."

Works Cited

Baer, Franklin C. Home page. 24 June 2000. <http//www.bemorecreative.com>.

Blakenship, Russell. American Literature As an Expression of the National Mind. Rev ed. New York: Cooper Square, 1973.

Bluestein, Gene. "Sex as a Literary Theme: Is Whitman the good, gay poet." Journal of Popular Culture Winter 1997: 153-162. Academic Search Elite. GALILEO. 18 Jun. 2000.

Callow, James T. and Reilly, Robert J. Guide to American Literature from its Beginnings through Walt Whitman. New York: Barnes, 1976.

Edwards, Jonathan. "Sinners in the Hands of an Angrey God." Lauter, et al., 598.

Erikkila, Betsy. 'Walt Whitman." Lauter, et al., 2725-28.

Lauter, Paul, et al., eds. The Heath Anthology of American Literature. Third ed. Boston: Houghton, 1998.

"Sayatasha's Night Chant." Lauter, et al., 74-93.

Smith, Gayle L. "Reading 'Song of Myself': Assuming What Whitman Assumes." ATQ Sept. 1992: 151-161. Academic Search Elite. GALILEO. 24 June 2000.

Valiunas, Algis. "I am the Man." Commentary (June 1999): 70-73. Academic Search Elite. GALILEO. 18 June 2000.

Vance, William. "What They're Saying About Whitman." Raritan Spring 1997: 127-152. Academic Search Elite. GALILEO. 18 June 2000.

Whitman, Walt. "Leaves of Grass". 1855 ed. Lauter et al., 2729-42.

----. "Song of Myself." 1855 ed. Lauter et al., 2743-94.

List of Contributors

Vanessa Arcio
Berkmar High School
Lilburn, GA

Santina Bennett
Marlboro High School
Marlboro, NJ

Shirley Bennett
Fillmore High School
Fillmore, CA

Adam Bost
Roswell High School
Roswell, GA

Courtney Branen
Parkview High School
Lilburn, GA

Frances Burke
Benjamin E. Mays High School
Atlanta, GA

Caroline Cahill
Ecole Classique
New Orleans, LA

William L. Carrillo
Iver C. Ranum High School
Denver, CO

Paula Clay
Gainesville, GA

Meseret Demissie
Bole High School
Addis Abeba, Ethiopia

Elizabeth Duckworth
Parkview High School
Lilburn, GA

Susan Fleming
Pickens High School
Jasper, GA

Sergio Gill
Chamblee, GA

Alexandra Hassiotis
Roswell High School
Roswell, GA

Jennifer S. Kaufman
Atlanta, GA

Mahfoudh Kayanda
Haileselassie Secondary
School
Zanzibar, Tanzania

Tracy Kirkpatrick
Atlanta, GA

Tatjana Krause
Fritz Erler Schule
Pforzheim, Germany

Cheryl Lea
North Clayton High School
College Park, GA

Terri-Ann Lee
Stephenson High School
Stone Mountain, GA

Claire Lunsford
Atlanta, GA

Ke Ma
Lawrenceville, GA

Angie D. Mabry
Sprayberry High School
Marietta, GA

Cora McCray
Chamblee High School
Chamblee, GA

Simone P. Mendez
St. Agostinho
Rio de Janeiro, Brazil

Henry Miller
Norcross High School
Norcross, GA

Adeline Mills
Irmo High School
Columbia, SC

Niki Neptune
Stone Mountain High School
Stone Mountain, GA

Sally Chase Palmer
North Springs High School
Atlanta, GA

Carmela Parish
Lakeside High School
Atlanta, GA

Meily Poon
Lakeside High School
Atlanta, GA

Daniel Proto
Meadowcreek High School
Norcross, GA

Mike Randazzo
Mill Springs Academy
Marietta, GA

Erreka Kenyarda Reed
Overton High School
Memphis, TN

Matthew J. Reese
Lake Braddock Secondary
  School, Burke, VA

Shelicia L. Reese
McNair High School
Atlanta, GA

Elena Resiga
Sibiu, Romania

Linda Rosenbaum
Mountain Brook High School
Birmingham, AL

Mendi Sandoz
Norcross High School
Norcross, GA

Fisnik Shpuza
Economics High School of
  Tirana, Tirana, Albania

Adam Sigelman
North Springs High School
Atlanta, GA

Shutida Srikanchana
Ekamai International School
Bangkok, Thailand

Jo Ann Terrell
Green County High School
Greensboro, GA

Cem Ultav
Shfal High School
Aydin, Turkey

Kali Williams
Norcross High School
Norcross, GA